The Wonderful Art of Drawing Horses

by
Barry Stebbing

How Great Thou ART Publications
Box 48 McFarlan, NC 28102
Copyright 2001
Revised Second Edition 2006
(Lessons within HGTA Publications are reproducible for *"in home use"* only)

The Wonderful Art of Drawing Horses

by
Barry Stebbing

"A Horse" by Vesta Elliott

Dedicated to: Every student who loves horses!

The Wonderful Art of Drawing Horses

Greetings Students;

First of all, let me begin by saying that I am not a horse artist. What I mean is, I couldn't draw horses very well before I began this book. One of the reasons I could not draw horses is because I never invested any time practicing how to drawing them. Oh, I had done some quick sketches of horses, but drawing horses was not something I had a strong desire to do or to learn more about.

Now, many years later, I have decided to create, "The Wonderful Art of Drawing Horses." There are several reasons for my new found interest in horses, one of which is that we have relocated to a farm in North Carolina where we have four horses: "Star," "Cheyenne," "Ginger," and "Little Bit." And, with this new life on the farm I began to sketch our horses in my art journals, thus finding a new love for drawing them. Secondly, many of the students whom we have instructed throughout the years across North America, have expressed a strong desire to learn how to draw horses. With this in mind, we would like to present to you, "The Wonderful Art of Drawing Horses."

However, before beginning, we want you to understand that you learn how to draw horses. Just like everything else in life it takes time, practice, understanding and determination. Remember, I was never a "horse artist." Deciding to teach myself to draw horses was the beginning of understanding and, with practice, led to much improvement in my horse drawings. The most wonderful lesson to be learned is that you, as a student of the fine arts and observer of the world around you, can be your own very best teacher. May we all learn and grow together.

We have also included many delightful horse drawings by homeschooling students within this text. This prolific gallery of horses should be inspiring and also allow you to see that we all have difficulty in the beginning. So, let's have fun and enjoy learning how to draw horses!

In Christ,

Stebbing

Barry Stebbing
How Great Thou ART Publications

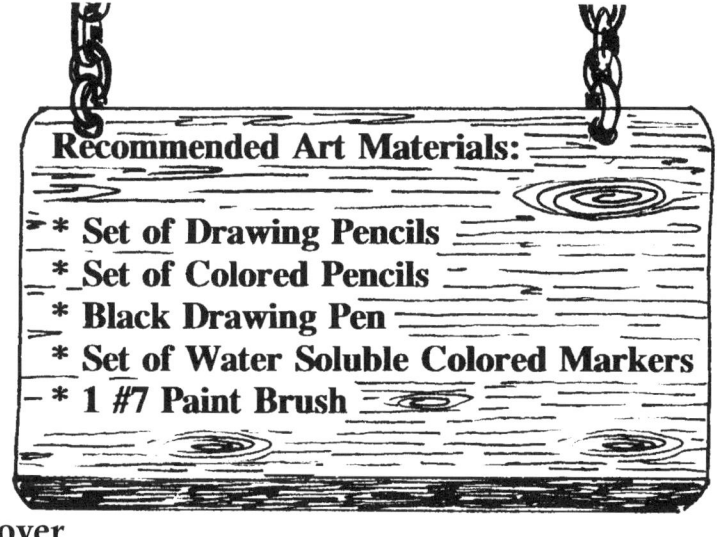

About the Cover
* Note: A special thanks to the students whose excellent horse drawings are on the front cover of *The Wonderful Art of Drawing Horses*. Matthew and Kristen Diaz's beautiful drawing to the left (#1), Rachel Taylor's wonderful horse in the upper right (#2), Maria Pecoraro's delightful horse in the bottom left (#3), and Lori Taylor's beautiful horse to the bottom right (#4). And, last of all, we thank Leonardo da Vinci, the great master of the Renaissance, for his wonderful sketch in the upper left. Thanks for a great job!

Lesson #1: *"Why I like horses"*

Before we start, it would be good for you to introduce yourself by writing a letter explaining why you enjoy horses. You have a choice in this letter: you may either write it to me, Barry Stebbing, telling me why you would like to learn to draw horses; or you can write a letter of introduction to all those who will open this book years from now, telling them why you love horses and why you desire to learn more about drawing them. In either case be descriptive. Do you like to ride horses? Do you think they are beautiful? Strong? Likeable? Do you have a horse? If not, would you like a horse? Why? Do you already know how to draw horses? What do you have the most difficulty with when drawing them? Do you know the different breeds of horses? If so, what is your favorite breed? Your favorite color for a horse? Finally, what is the name of your horse or the name you would give a horse if you owned one? Write your letter below. Practice good penmanship. Stay in the lines. Use correct grammar and punctuation. After all, God is watching you.

Dear evryon including Bery Stebbing

I am Jessica But you can call me Jess Not Jessie. I love horses becuse 1# I love to ride horses. 2# I want something that is a lovadul thing to take care of but also something that can protect me. I would love a horse becuse its strong nice and I could train him to do almost enything I want to do. and I have alwase loved drawing so I thogt why not give THIS a try. my favoret breed of all tim HAS to be a small halsny. my favoret coler for a bigger horse is a handsam chesnt. my favoret coler for a halsny is a white blck mix. the name of my halsny if... if I got one would Be Back   white   whiteBlck mix   chesnut.
twilight   star   stoopy   calico

Table of Contents

I. Beginning Drawing   Lessons #2 thru #39   Page 11

A great chapter for the beginning student. Many basic lessons on drawing horses along with other creative art lessons. Filled with "how to" illustrations and a variety of student horse examples of drawings.

II. Intermediate Horse Drawing   Lessons #40 thru #66   Page 55

This chapter brings the student to a slightly higher level in learning how to draw horses. Lessons on anatomy, various angles of drawing a horse, copying from a picture, drawing from life, shading and adding values from light to dark, and more.

III. Horse Artists   Lessons #67 thru 81   Page 89

This chapter discusses many of the great horse artists throughout history such as the great American Western artists, Charles Russell and Frederick Remington; the French artist, Eugene Delacroix; the English artist, George Stubbs; and the great Renaissance master, Leonardo da Vinci. Many illustrations by these masters and various lessons.

IV. Colored Markers   Lessons #82 thru 87   Page 109

Delightful lessons on how to color horses with colored markers! This chapter includes five *marker cards* which are used for the colored marker assignments. Students will learn about the color wheel, coloring with lines, blending, and working from light to dark.

V. Sketchbook   Page 119

A small sketchbook has been provided in the back of the text for some of the student's drawings along with several pointers on drawing and how to keep a sketchbook.

Student ART Gallery

"Horse Rearing" by Luke Adams Age 13

"Running Wild" by Jennifer Martura Age 10

"Wild Stallion" by Sarah Northrop Age 12

"Horse in Action" by Lily Knights Age 16

"Stallion" by Morgan McClananhan Age 14

"Running Free" by Rachael Wardyn Age 12

The Wonderful Art of Drawing Horses

Part I
Beginning Horse Drawing

"Ride 'em Cowboy" by David Margulis Age 12

"In the beginning God created horses and said it was good."
Barry Stebbing

Lesson #2: *My Horse*

Now that you have written your thoughts about horses, describing why you like them, let's attempt to draw a horse in the figure box below. Don't worry if you can't draw a horse! We are only asking that you try. The purpose of this lesson is to see how you draw a horse before beginning the text.

Use your colored pencils to draw and color your horse. Also, draw and color a red barn in the distance, a green pasture, a fence, some flowers in the foreground, and a sunny sky. Draw your horse in profile (sideways) either looking to the left or to the right. Draw his head, entire body, all four legs, and hooves. When finished, give your horse a name and place the date above your drawing.

Finally, write about your horse on the lines below. Does it look like a horse? What do you like about your drawing? What parts of the body did you have the most difficulty with? Is your horse funny looking? Does it look more like a donkey? A dog? A large rabbit? Remember, we all start off as beginners, and everyone begins by making funny looking horses.

My Horse's Name is: _____   Date: _____

_____
_____
_____
_____
_____

"And thus I saw the horses in the vision..." Revelation 9:17

Lesson #3: *Having Fun with Horses*

As you probably know, it is not easy drawing horses. Many students, when first attempting to draw them, make horses look like all kinds of strange and funny creatures, such as long legged giraffes, dogs, hippopotamuses, moose, or even large bunny rabbits. However, art is to be enjoyed, and even if your first horse turns out to be kind of funny looking, simply enjoy the act of creating! Date your horse drawings and see how much you learn as you continue to practice. Remember, art should be enjoyable, and the more you practice the better you will do. For this assignment, take the horse you drew in Lesson #2 and add it to the gallery of student horse drawings by drawing him or her in the picture frame on page 9. Use your black drawing pen for this assignment.

Student Artwork: Kayla Dewitt Age 10

Student Artwork: Josh O'Neal Age 8

Student Artwork: Deanna Tylee Age 6

Student Gallery

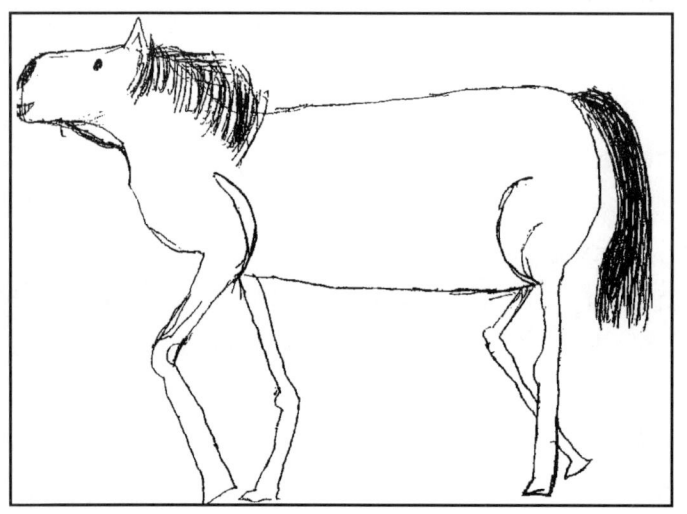
Michael Harmon Age 10

Jessica Lee Collins Age 8

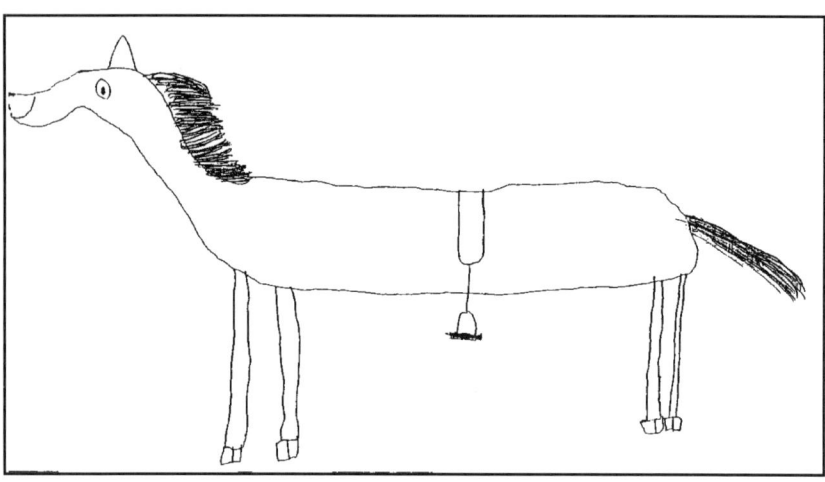
Tyler DeWitt Age 6

Amanda Nelson Age 9

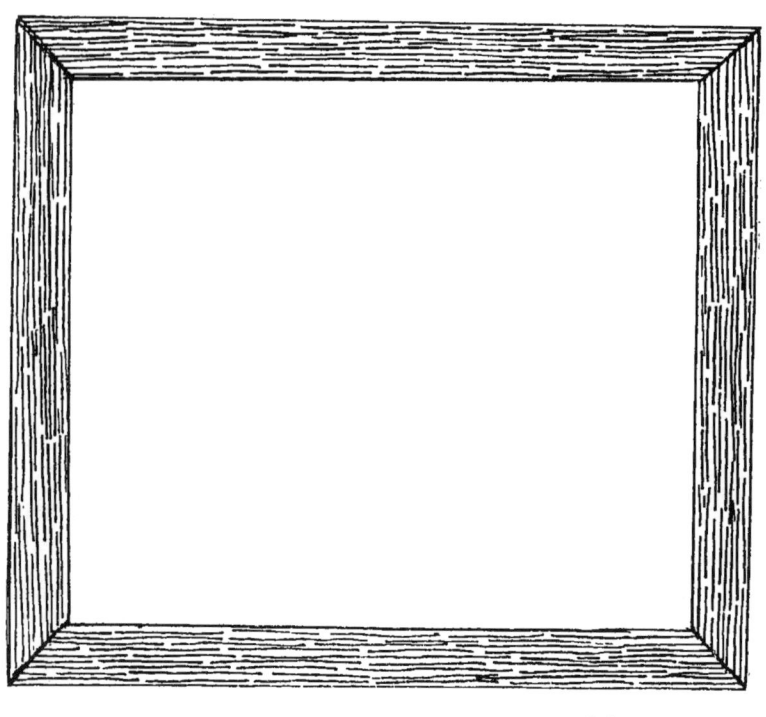

Lesson #4: *Shading with Lines*

There are two ways to shade in your drawings. One is by smudge shading, and the other is by shading with lines. In this text, we are going to teach you to shade with lines. Basically, there are four different ways of shading with lines: *horizontal, vertical, diagonal,* or *cross-hatching* (A). Each method can create a different effect, and most students prefer one type of shading with lines over another. For example, I like to shade with diagonal lines in my drawings (see page 71). Notice the drawing below by Lydia Wood and how she shaded mostly with horizontal lines (B). Also, notice the horse drawing by Nicolas Iocco below and how he shaded mostly with cross-hatching (C).

A.

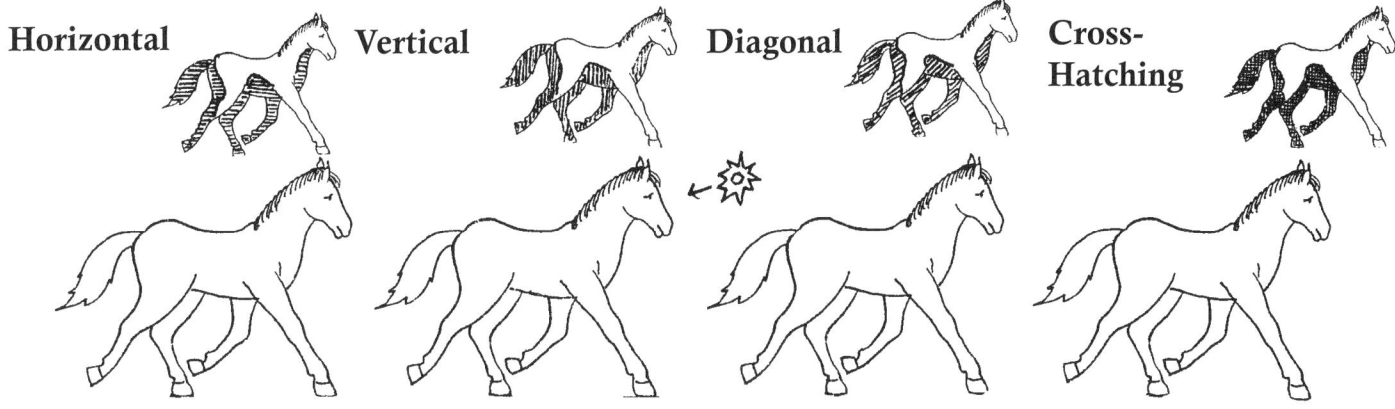

B. Shading with Horizontal Lines

"*Horse Study*" Lydia Wood Age 12

C. Shading with Cross-Hatching

light source

"*Grazing Horse*" Nicolas Iocco Age 15

D.

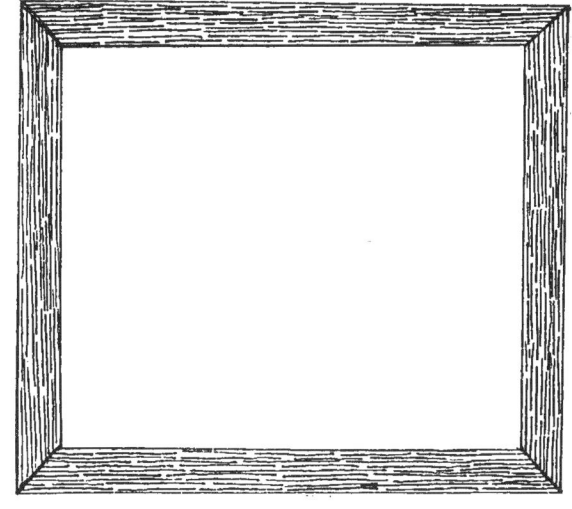

For this assignment, shade the four horses above, shading one with horizontal lines, one with vertical lines, one with diagonal lines, and the last with cross-hatching. Can you shade the parts of each horse as illustrated in the top row (above)? Use a *2B* or *3B* pencil for this.

Finally, in the picture frame to the left (D) draw a horse with a light source (showing the light coming from a certain direction and drawing a little arrow as shown above). Then shade your horse with your *5B* pencil and use your favorite type of shading with lines from the examples above.

Lesson #5: *A Horse Named "Spot"*

A. Pinto

B. Spotted Horse

Have you ever seen a horse with spots? A horse with spots is called either a *Pinto* or *Spotted*. A Pinto's coat usually has large spots of brown, black, or white (A). A Spotted horse generally has smaller spots of brown or black on the rump or spread over the entire body (B).

For this assignment, draw large spots on the first horse below (C), coloring them in black or brown (leave some white) to make a *Pinto*. Then, on the second horse (D), draw smaller spots on either the rump or the entire horse and color them in to make a *Spotted* horse. Finally, in your sketchbook, draw the entire horse and make it either a *"Pinto"* or a *"Spotted"* horse.

C. Pinto

"Painted Pinto" by Rebekah Lorenz Age 10

D. Spotted

"Galloping Spotted Horse" by Gray Goodner Age 8

Notice the drawing (above left) of the Pinto by Rebekah Lorenz and how delightful the large spots are which she put on her horse. Notice also that she left black areas against white (the two front legs). This will allow you to show the form of the horse better and not get lost in all the dark areas. Now observe the "Galloping Spotted Horse" (left) by Gray Goodner, and observe how his spots are much smaller.

Lesson #6: *A Horse is a Horse*

For this assignment, trace the horse to the right (A) into the picture frame on the next page (page 18), which is situated exactly in the same place as this one. Observe that there is a third picture frame on the following page (page 19) that is also located in the same position as the one on this page. We are going to trace the horse to the right through the "carbon" we are going to make on page 18 and into the picture frame on page 19. First, take your *5B* pencil and lay a flat, toned layer of pencil inside the picture frame on page 18. This is done by holding the side of your pencil as shown (B). Make sure the entire figure box is covered with a flat, even layer of pencil lead. Now you have a carbon for copying the horse in the picture frame.

A.

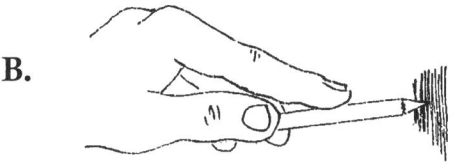
B.

Finally, take the point of your *HB* pencil and trace over the horse above (A), transferring through your carbon and into the picture frame on the top of page 19.

Lesson #7: *Horse Sense*

Look at the basic shape of a horse (C). It has a hump over the shoulder and also for the rump, or *"croup,"* (krup). The rear thigh and the front forearm of the horse (top part of each leg) taper down in a wide funnel shape as illustrated. The bottom of each leg is like a long, thin rectangle.

Can you see that the hooves go out at an angle? For this assignment, draw the basic shape of the horse in the picture frame using your *5B* drawing pencil.

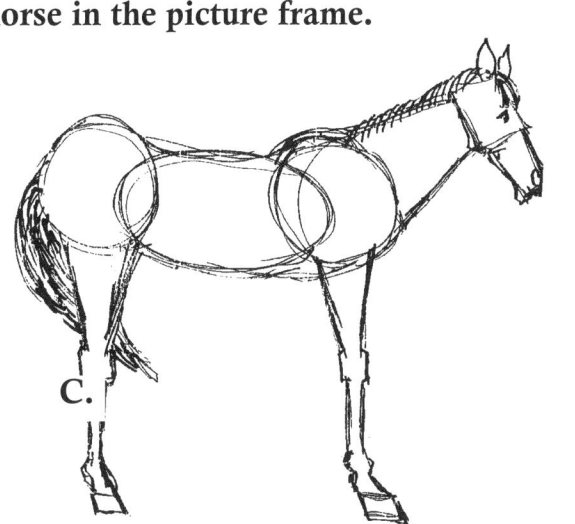
C.

Lesson #8: *Drawing a Horse*

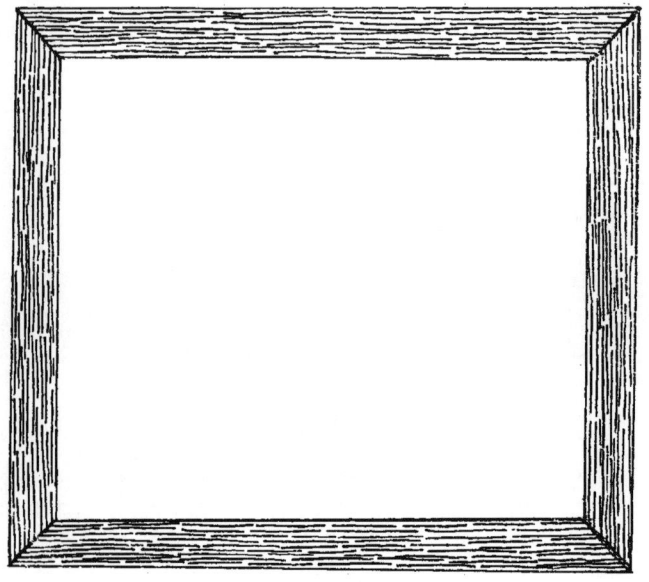

Let's draw the horse by copying it's body in the figure box below. First, complete the rest of the horse in A. Notice the head, tail, and hooves are already drawn. All you have to do is complete the rest of the body. Remember, there is a slight dip in the horse's back between the rear hump and the shoulders. Likewise, the top part of the legs, or thighs, are thicker than the bottom part of the legs (as shown in the previous lesson). Use your HB pencil to start. Then, when you have completed your drawing, go over your horse with your black drawing pen. Finally, draw and color some large spots on your horse.

When you have finished, draw the entire horse in the picture frame provided (B). Start your drawing with your yellow colored pencil, and then go over it with your other colored pencils. You may want to try blending several colors together. Can you make a nice brown by mixing colors? Practice mixing browns in the circles below. (Take a peak at page 29 for some helpful hints).

A. Complete the Horse   **B. Draw Your Horse Here**

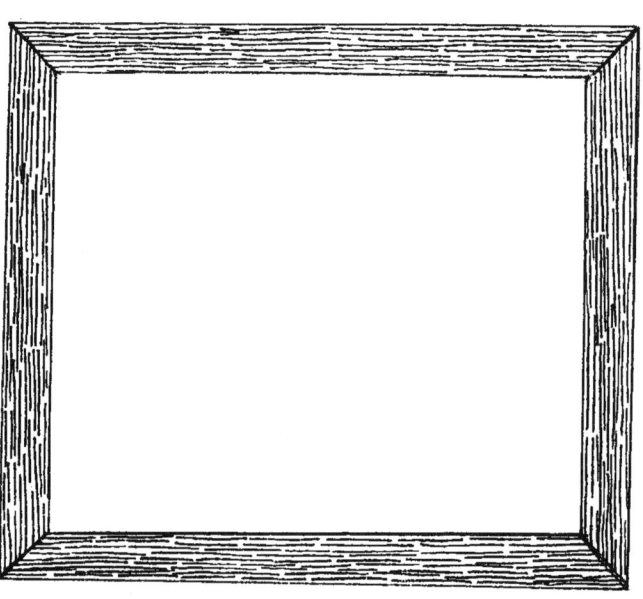

Brown - Brown - Brown

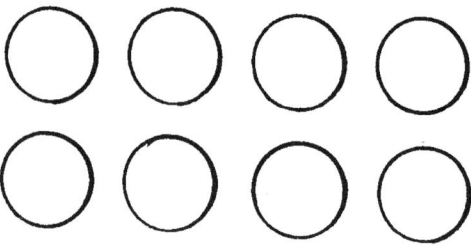

"Horse Drawing" by Olivia Gover Age 11

Lesson #9: *Drawing a Horse*

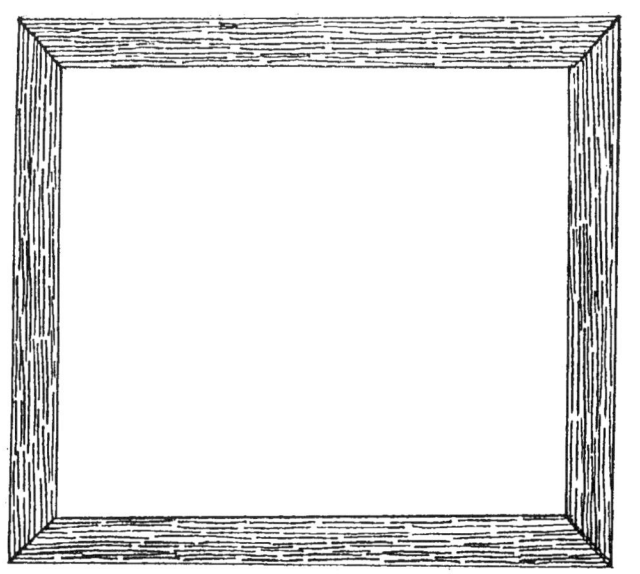

Let's draw our horse again from Lesson #6. This time, do your drawing in your sketchbook, drawing him step-by-step. First, draw a fairly large oval for the stomach area of the horse (A). Then draw a circle going through each end of your oval for the horse's *croup* (rump) and shoulder (B). For the top part of his *thigh* (rear leg) and *forearm* (front leg) draw a trapezoid (C). Have you ever noticed the two large knobs that protrude from a horse's leg? They are similar to our kneecaps and ankles. On the rear leg, this know is called the *"hook"* and on the foreleg it is simply called the *"knee."*

The other knob, further down, near the ankle on each leg is called the *"fetlock."* Simply draw a small, curved rectangular shape for this area that protrudes at the horse's knee and ankle (D & E). The hoof is created by drawing a *parallelogram* at the end of each leg. As mentioned, a parallelogram is like a slanted square, as all the sides are the same size but two are slanted in the same direction (F). Notice that I have drawn the horse's leg (below) using a trapezoid for the thigh, a thin rectangle for the bottom of the leg, curved rectangles for the knee and ankle, and a parallelogram for the hoof (G). The tail is drawn in a curved, cone shape that comes to a point and the details are put in like a waterfall. Finally, add your horse's head to the body, and you have your horse! Start with your yellow pencil to draw the basic shapes. Then, go over everything with your brown pencil in some areas and your black pencil in other areas (the eyes, hooves, nose, ears, and tail). Before beginning, you may want to take a plain sheet of white paper and trace over the horse below to have a better idea of all the shapes.

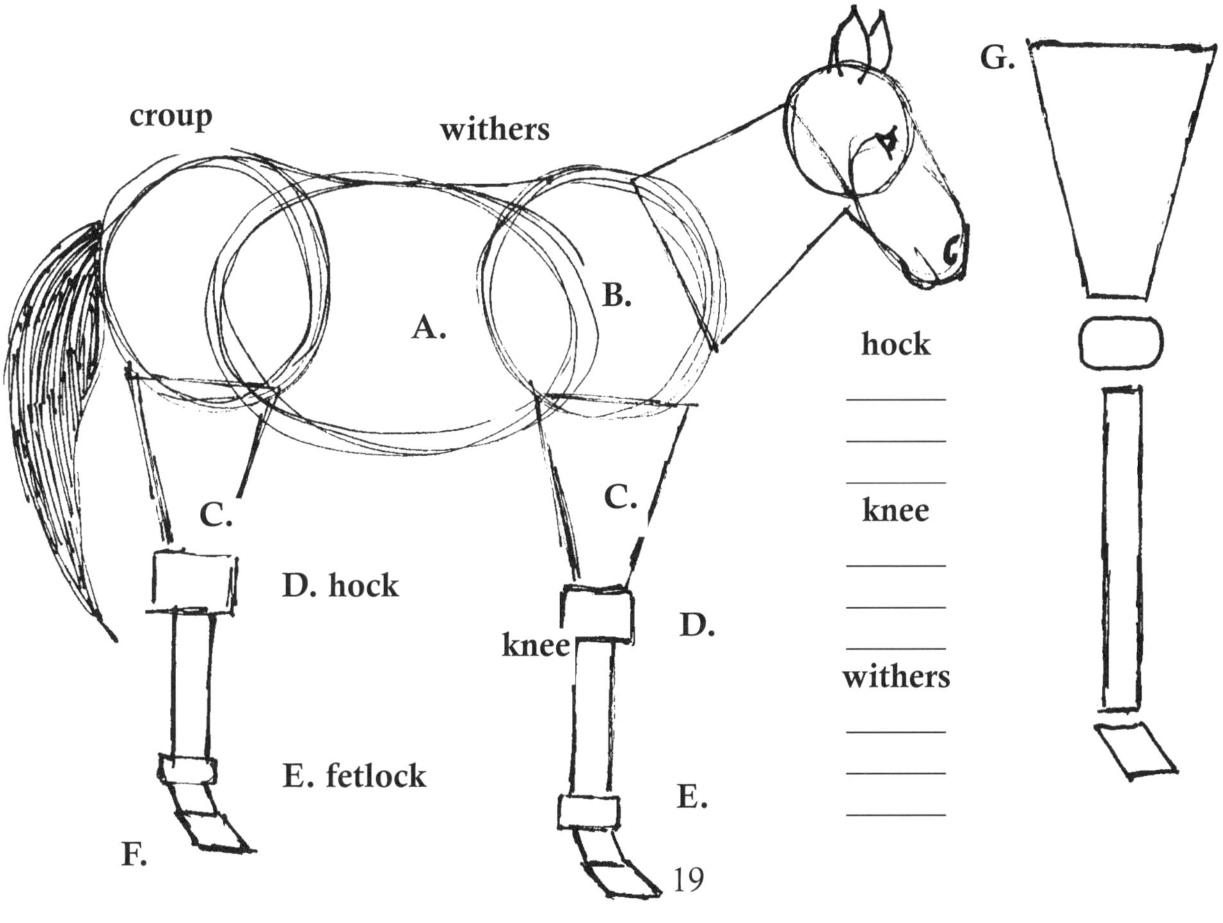

Lesson #10: *Basic Fundamentals*

Basic *"fundamentals"* are building blocks in art. These fundamentals should be practiced and learned in order to improve one's drawing abilities. There are fundamentals for learning everything from how to play baseball, to how to draw, paint, and even ride a horse! For this lesson, let's practice some of these fundamentals again, which are important in beginning horse drawing. We first practiced some of these in Lesson #7 for the various shapes of a horse. For example, learning how to draw an oval is very important in drawing the basic shape of the horse's belly (A). Likewise, learning how to draw a circle is important for drawing the shoulder and the *croup*, along with the basic shape for the top of a horse's head (B).

A.

B.

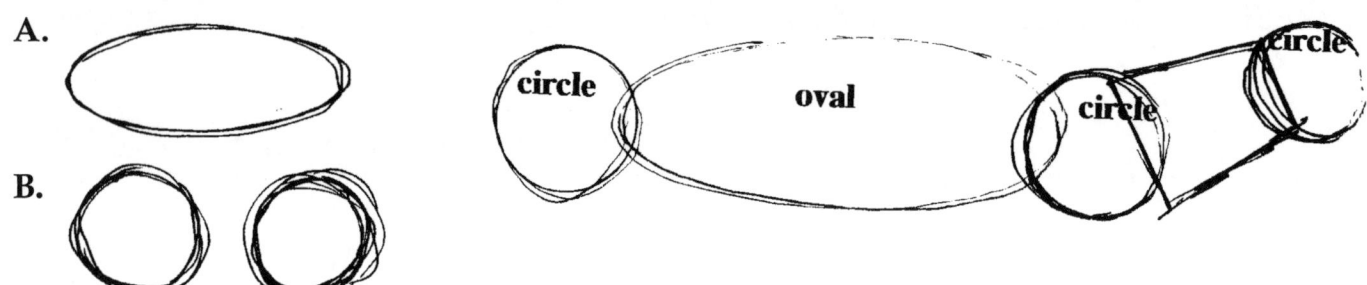

C. trapezoid

E. horse's leg

There are several other important shapes to learn when first drawing a horse. One is a *"trapezoid."* This is a shape with four straight lines, like a square. However, two of the lines come in close together to make the shape thinner at one end, like a funnel (C). A rectangle is a shape that is also similar to a square, with four straight sides. Each side is parallel to the one across from it as they go in exactly the same direction. But, unlike a square, one side of the rectangle is longer than the other (D). A thin rectangular shape and a tapering trapezoid combine together to give you the basic shape of a horse's leg from top to bottom (E). Finally, notice the hoof is shaped like a *"parallelogram,"* where all four sides are parallel but two sides are on a slant.

D. rectangle   F. parallelogram

Draw these basic shapes (oval, circle, trapezoid, parallelogram, and thin rectangle) three times each in the figure box below or in your sketchbook. You may want to trace over each shape before beginning to have a better idea of how to draw them. Remember, a circle is round, keep your ovals wide, and the lines for your rectangles and trapezoids are straight.

The horse drawing below (A) was done by a 6 year old student in one of our art classes. She used the various geometric shapes to draw it as you did in the previous lesson. Even though her horse looks a little strange, Kelsey did not do too bad putting the parts together. The circles for the shoulder and croup should be a little larger than she drew them, but the rest of her horse looks pretty good. Remember, after this first step of drawing in all the basic shapes you need to round off everything (B), which will make the horse look more realistic.

A. Student Drawing Using Geometric Shape   **B. Student Drawing Rounded Off**

"A Horse"
by Kelsey Raelee
Age 6

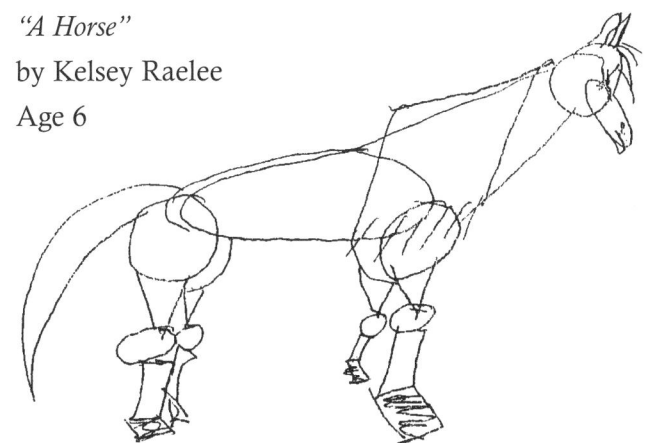
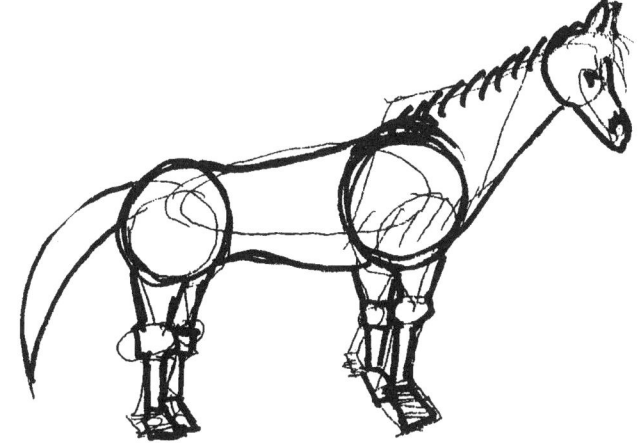

Lesson #11: *Completing a Picture*

Let's see if you can now draw the horse from page 19 on your own. Take out your colored pencils and draw the picture of the traced horse as shown below (C). First, lightly draw it in with your yellow colored pencil, and then color it in with other colors. Complete the picture by placing a green hill behind your horse, some flowers in the foreground, a light blue sky with a cloud, and the sun. When you are finished, sign your picture with your best *artistic signature* in the bottom right-hand corner with a colored pencil.

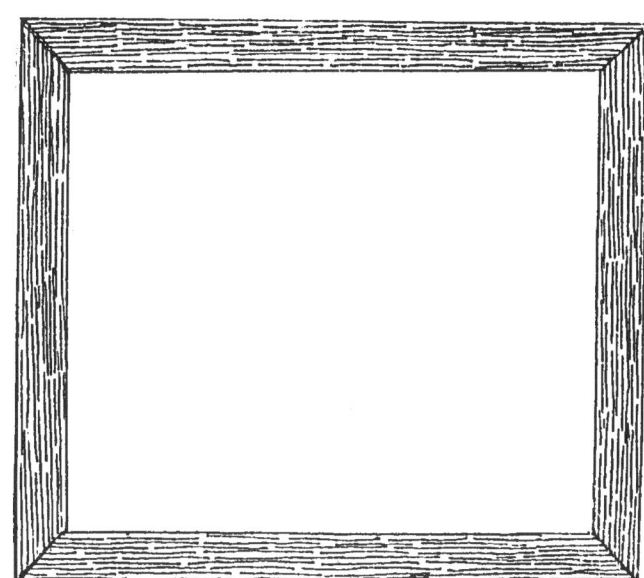

C.

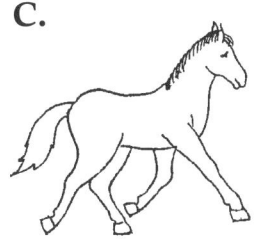

Practice writing your artistic signature three times on the lines below. You can print or write your first name and last initial, or your first initial and last name. Whichever method you choose, have a nice artistic signature, write it small, and use a color that is in your picture. Notice how I practiced signing my artistic signature until I created a signature I liked the best (below).

Practice Your Artistic Signature

Lesson #12: *Learning the Parts of a Horse*

Several parts of a horse are listed below (A). Take a look at them and try to remember each as we will be using some of these terms throughout the text. First, neatly write or print the three words ten times each on the lines provided: *withers, fetlock,* and *croup*. These are important terms to learn when drawing a horse. Finally, draw the horse in the space below (B) and neatly label the parts shown. However, this time draw the horse from memory. Study the drawing below, then cover it up and see if you can draw it on your own.

A.

withers

fetlock

B.

croup

Lesson #13: *Drawing by Valerie*

One day, my 8 year old niece, Valerie, came to visit our farm. Valerie loves to draw horses, so we took our sketchbooks and went out to the barn to sketch *Star* and *Cheyenne*. Below is Valerie's first drawing of one of the horses (A). It is certainly a lovely horse, however, if she had started with a few of the basic shapes, her horse would have a more true to life structure.

So, I gave Valerie a basic lesson in drawing horses using geometric shapes and this is what she did (B). Now her second horse is certainly a great improvement, don't you agree? I'm sure if she continues to remember some of these pointers that her horse drawings will improve and look more realistic. For example, Valerie had some problems drawing the *round* circles for the shoulder and the rump along with having a little difficulty drawing the trapezoid for the wider, upper part of the horse's legs. Remember, drawing these basic shapes takes practice.

A. Valerie's First Horse **B. Valerie's Second Horse**

Copy the horse below (C) in the figure box on the bottom of the page (D). Use the basic shapes as shown. However, this time, see if you can draw your horse looking in the opposite direction (from right to left instead of left to right). Start your drawing off lightly with your *HB* pencil and then, when you have drawn all the shapes correctly, go over your horse with your *5B* drawing pencil, smoothing out some of the areas.

D. Looking This Way

C.

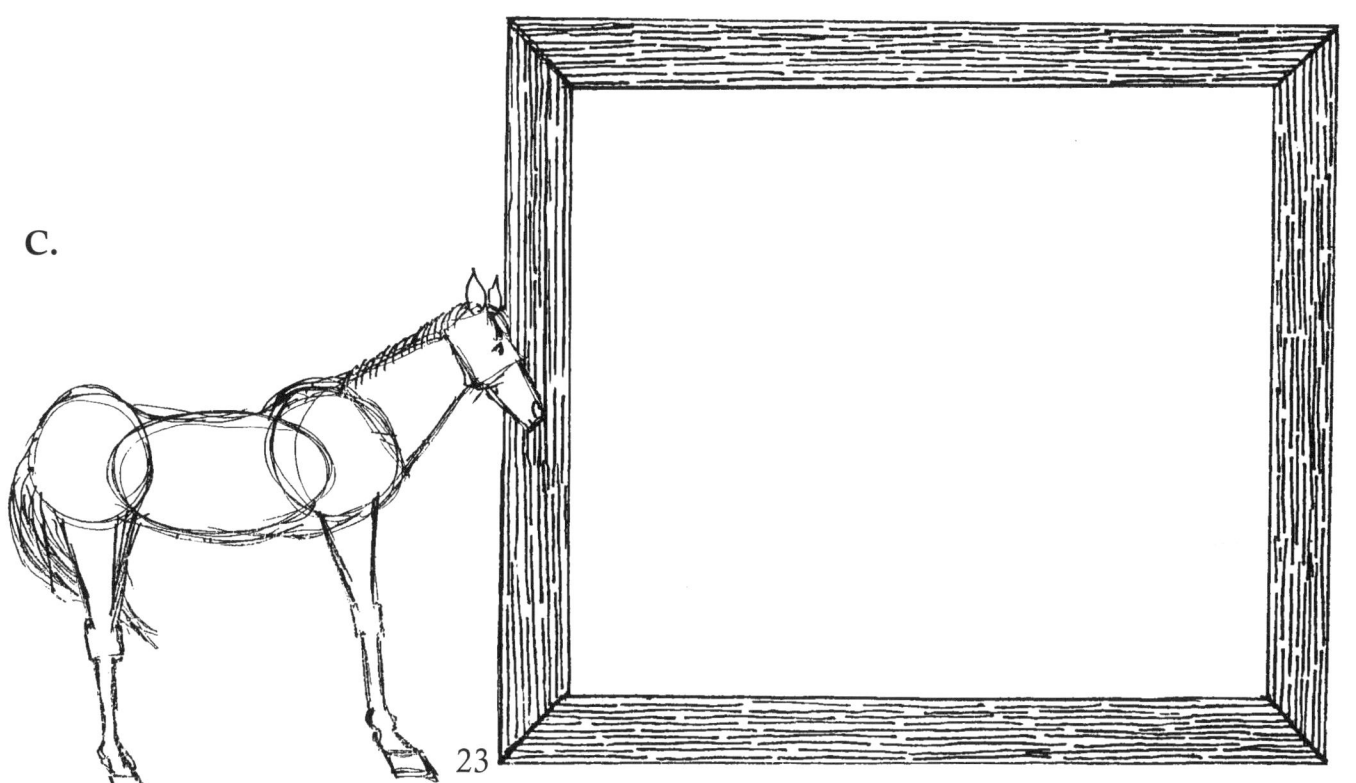

Lesson #14: *Connect the Leg Bone to the Thigh Bone...*

A. Thigh

B. Long Rectangle

C. Hoof

D. *"Hock"*

E. *"Fetlock"*

F.

One of the most important parts of a horse to draw is the leg. It is essential and not that difficult to draw. The thigh (the top part of the horse's leg) is thicker than the bottom part. Start by drawing a trapezoid for the thigh (A). The bottom part of the leg, as mentioned, is a fairly long, thin rectangle (B). This part of the horse's leg is called the *"cannon."* If the horse is looking forward, the hoof becomes a trapezoid and not a parallelogram (C).

As you have learned in Lesson #9, there are also two large knots on the horse's leg. The top knot on the rear leg (between the thigh and the bottom part of the leg) is the *"hock"* (D). However, it is called the *"knee"* on the front leg. The other knot is on the bottom of each leg where it joins the hoof (like the ankle of a horse). This is called the *"fetlock"* (E). After drawing these basic shapes, smooth them out by removing some of the straight lines and lumps as illustrated in the leg below (F). For this assignment, draw the legs on the two horses below, one from a front view and the other from a side view. Start with the basic shapes and then smooth them out.

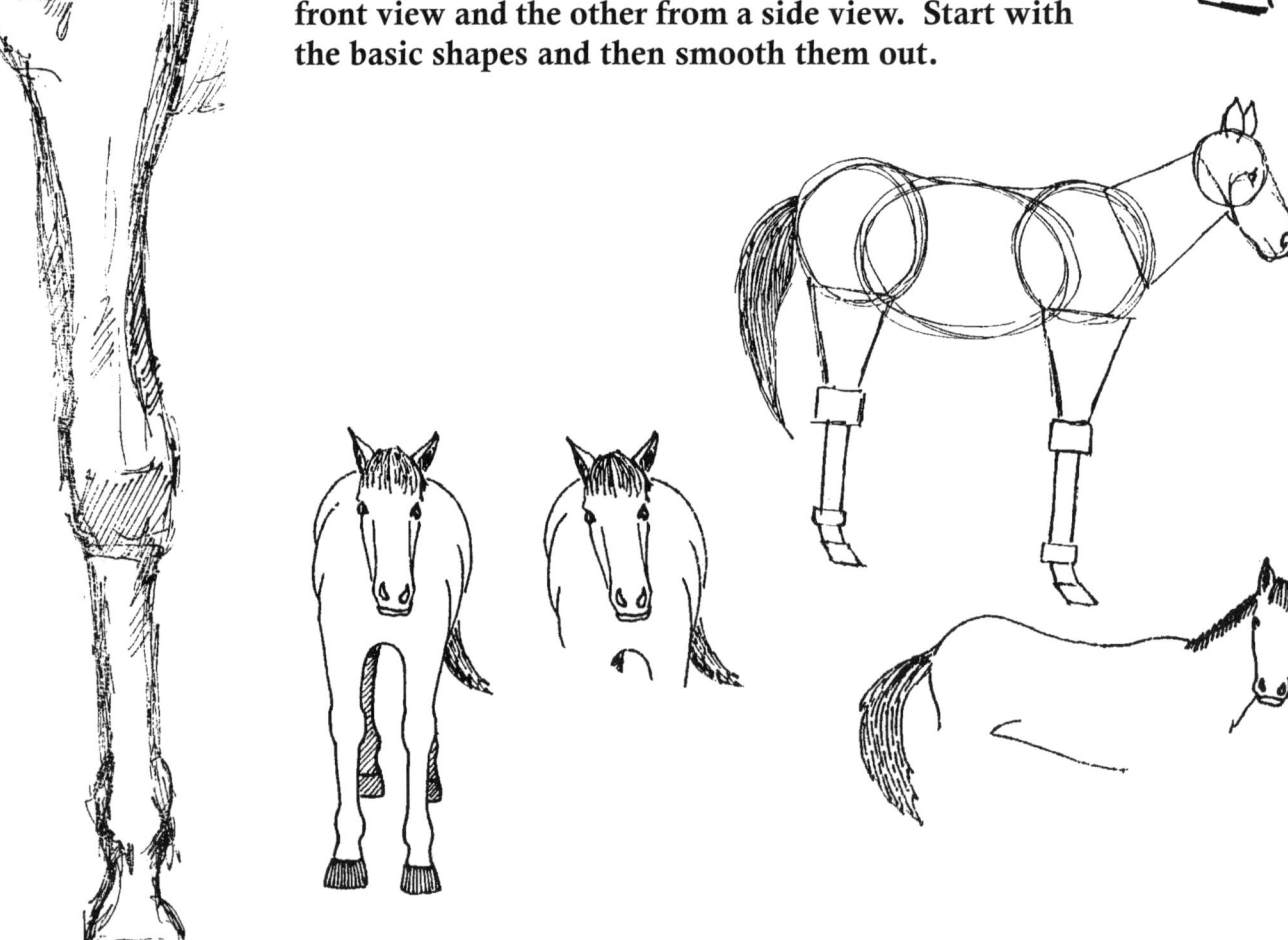

A.

"Horse" by Eleanor Harmon Age 9

Lesson #15: *Proper Positioning of Legs*

A common mistake made by many students is that they draw all the legs the same length. Notice the delightful drawing by Eleanor (A). She certainly drew a nice horse. However, notice that all the legs are the same length. In reality, the two legs on the far side of the horse should be shorter because they are more in the distance. Notice what happens when I shorten the two far legs (B). The horse seems to stand better. In your drawings of horses, the far legs always have to be shorter than the legs that are closer to you. This will show depth in your drawing (C). Finally, you may want to shade the far legs to add more depth and because there is usually shade under the belly of the horse.

Turn back to the previous lesson and observe your drawing. How do your legs look? For this lesson, draw a horse in the picture frame below (D). Draw all four legs including the different shapes and parts. Make sure the two far legs are shorter than the legs closest to you. Use your *HB* pencil for this assignment and then go over it with your black drawing pen.

B.

D. Draw Your Horse Here

C.

Horse Sense
Legs on the far side of a horse have to be shorter.

Lesson #16:
Drawing a Horse's Head in Profile

Let's now learn how to draw a horse's head. First, draw a circle for his forehead (A). Next, draw an oval that goes through the circle and extends down for the nose (B). (Do not make this oval shape too thin.) Next, the horse's nose comes in at a slant as shown. Draw a line for his mouth and a small circle for the bottom lip, or chin (C).

The nostril is like an upside down tear drop, and the end of his nose and mouth are shaded to make them darker (D). The eye is located where the circle joins the top of the oval. For the eye, start with a very simple shape like a bird flying sideways and draw a half-circle in it (E). The ears are drawn like porpoise fins (F) with another curved line coming down to show the opening of the ear (G). This opening in the ear is then shaded (H). The part of the mane between the ears and over the forehead (*forelock*) is drawn with short, curved strokes (I).

A. B. C. D. E. F. G. H.

I.

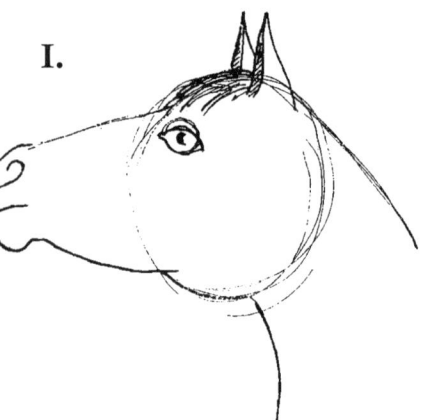

J. **Draw Your Horse's Head Here**

Do not forget to draw a little ball shape for the chin, and then round off the nose and the bottom of the head with curved lines.

Observe the horse's head to the left by Natalie Sheda. It is a good drawing as she has most of the shapes and features drawn correctly. I especially like the way the neck, *forelock,* and ear were drawn. Draw your horse's head in the figure box above (J). Use your yellow pencil and draw the horse step-by-step. When you have finished, outline your horse with your black colored pencil.

"Profile of Horse" by Natalie Sheda Age 11

A.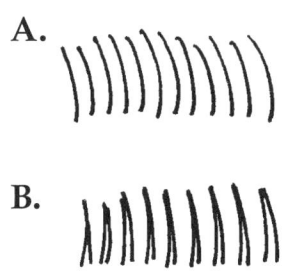

B.

Lesson #17: *Drawing Grass & Manes*

Horses and grass go hand-in-hand. (You can't have one without the other!) Today, let's learn how to draw grass and the mane of a horse since they can be drawn in a similar manner. Many students draw with skinny lines to make stick figures, very thin flower stems, and skinny blades of grass.

C.

Sometimes it is best to use a double line to show thickness, especially when drawing grass or the mane of a horse. Instead of drawing a single line (A), draw two, slightly curved lines that become thinner as they come to a point (B). Notice the delightful horse drawn by Heidi and how she used double lines coming to a curved point for the mane (D). For this assignment, use your black pen to practice drawing grass between the two flowers (C), and also a mane on the horse (E). Finally, in the figure box below, draw a horse in a pasture with grass beneath his feet, using double lines for the grass and mane.

D. Artwork by Heidi Hempel Age 12

E.

Lesson #18: *Drawing A Horse Part II*

Let's learn a few more pointers to improve our horse drawings. First of all, the neck of a horse is curved and goes under the foreleg, connecting with the curve of the bottom of the belly as Josh Killinger correctly illustrated to the left (A). The part where the neck connects with the belly is called the *breast*. Secondly, there is a slight sag in the back between the two humps. Many younger students make the horse's back flat, as in Eleanor's adorable horse (B).

"A Horse" by Josh Killinger Age 16

Now look at the delightful horse drawing by Hudson Mann (C). Notice that the breast was drawn correctly, but that it does not connect with a nice curve to the neck. However, he did draw the slight sag in the back correctly, as well as the four legs, even though they were all drawn the same length. (Remember, the back legs are more in the distance and need to be a little shorter.) Draw the horse below in the figure box (D), making the proper corrections by connecting the neck to the belly, the back sag between the two humps, and the far legs a little shorter.

"Horse Sketch" by Eleanor Davis Age 7

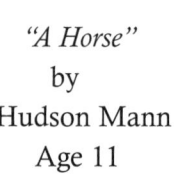

"A Horse" by Hudson Mann Age 11

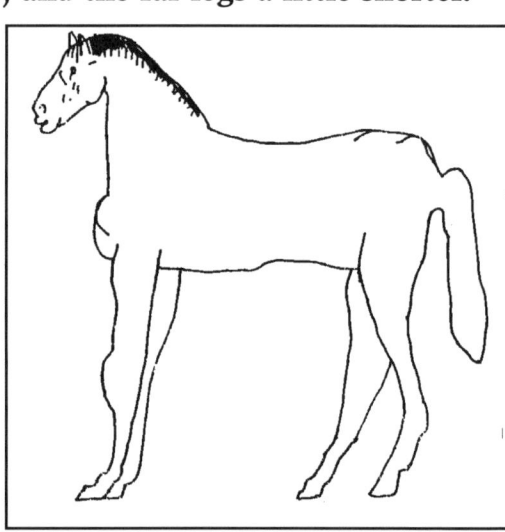

Draw Your Horse Here D.

"My purpose is, indeed, a horse of that color." William Shakespeare

Lesson #19: *A Horse of a Different Color*

Many students simply color their horses brown. However, there are many wonderful colors you can color a horse. We have just mentioned *"Pinto"* and *"Spotted"* colored horses. Do you know what color a *"Dun"* is? How about a *"Bay?"* What color is a *"Chestnut?"* A *"Gray?"* Or a *"Palomino?"*

A.

"Horse Study" Whit Knight Age 9

A *"Dun"* can vary in color from a mouse gray to a sandy color, and generally has a black mane, tail, and legs. A *"Bay"* is generally a light reddish/brown color (more brown than red), and also has a black mane and tail. However, only the bottom part of each leg is black. A *"Chestnut"* is also reddish/brown in color (very little red), and it's mane, tail, and legs are the same color as the body. A *"Gray"* can vary from white to a dark gray and can also be dappled with spots, but the basic undertone of the skin is black (so you would want to color it in lightly with black first before adding the gray or spots). A *"Palomino"* is a gold color (yellow with a slight touch of orange) and sometimes has a white mane and tail.

Do you know how to mix and create colorful browns with you colored pencils? Yellow, red, and a little green make a nice brown. Orange and violet with a little red also makes a colorful brown. Try orange, red, and a touch of blue. You can even make new browns by adding various amounts of yellow, violet, red, or even a little blue to your brown with your colored pencils. There are many ways to make delightful browns. For this assignment, use your colored pencils to color in the horse by Whit Knight at the top of the page (A). Then color the row below (B) with different colors of browns, grays, and tans. Finally, on the bottom row (C), see if you can color a *"Bay," "Chestnut," "Dun,"* and *"Palomino,"* and print the type of horse it is on the lines provided.

B.

C. *"Bay"* *"Chestnut"* *"Dun"* *"Palomino"*

A.

three hands

two hands

one hand

Lesson #20: *Horses & Ponies*

Do you know how to measure a horse? It is helpful to know the size of a horse when describing it and also for riding gear. A horse is measured by "*hands.*" A *hand* is the average size of the width of the four fingers of a man's hand (A). To measure a horse, start from the hoof and measure up to the withers (near the top of the shoulders).

"A Strong Horse" by David Fischer Age 15

Do you know the difference between a horse and a pony? A pony can vary in size up to 14.2 hands. However, a horse is larger than a pony. There are many varieties, or *"breeds,"* of horses just as there are many breeds of dogs, such as collies, poodles, terriers, etc. Some breeds of horses are: *Mustang, Appaloosa, Clydesdale, Palomino, American Saddle Horse, Quarter Horse,* and *Thoroughbred*. Besides its size, each breed of horse has certain characteristics that make it unique, such as strong legs, a thick neck, a short nose, or even long hair.

The *Percheron* is a breed of horse originally from France. This is a working horse that is known for its strength, and is either gray or black in color. Notice the Percheron by Carrie Ann (below). It certainly looks like a strong, working horse, doesn't it? There are many other breeds of horses including *Ponies of America* with its long tail, as wonderfully illustrated by Terri Sollie.

Now look at the powerful horse by David Fisher above. Quite possibly it is a Morgan, which is a well built, muscular horse. The Morgan's head is a little shorter than other breeds. It also has a thick neck. These unique traits are what distinguishes it from other horses and ponies.

For this assignment, go to the library and research the various breeds of horses. Then draw three of your favorites in your sketchbook, and write why you like these breeds. If you do not have access to a book on the different horse breeds, simply copy the three horses on this page drawn by other students.

"Percheron" by Carrie Ann Mann Age 10

"Ponies of America" by Terry Sollie

Lesson #21: *Shetland Ponies*

As mentioned, ponies are shorter than horses. The *"Shetland Pony"* is well-loved by children with its adorable, shaggy appearance. Not only is it smaller than a regular horse, but also stocky, similar to the Morgan and Percheron, only smaller. However, the greatest trait of a Shetland pony is the hairy legs near the hooves. Notice the delightful Shetland ponies by Andrew and Meghan below.

"Shetland Pony" by Andrew Ross Age 12   *"Shetland Pony"* by Meghan Atchison Age 9

If you look closely, you will find that many horses have differently shaped legs. The shape of their legs helps them adapt to the labors they perform. Thin legs mean more speed, whereas larger, sturdier legs are support for the heavier weight of larger horses. Observe below how sturdy the Shetland pony's legs are and how you can barely see the joints. Also, notice the thickness of the neck and the large volume of the belly, shoulders, and rump. For this assignment, draw the Shetland pony in the figure box with your *HB* pencil and then go over it with a darker pencil when finished. Have the sunlight coming from the upper right. Use lighter lines on the light side of the horse and darker lines on the shaded side. (In some areas you may not even need a line.) Finally, do not forget the shaggy feet.

Lesson #22: *Horse Markings*

No two snowflakes are alike and horses, like everything else God has created, have unique *"markings"* that can specifically identify each. Besides the color or build of a horse, facial features and markings can also help us to identify individual horses.

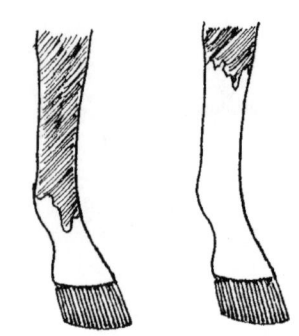

A. Sock B. Stocking

For this exercise, let's learn about leg markings. If the very bottom part of the leg, from the hoof to the *"fetlock joint,"* is white, it is called a *"sock"* (A). However, if the white *"sock"* goes up the *"cannon"* (the long, rectangular shape below the knee), the marking is called a *"stocking"* (B). For the first part of this assignment, draw a *"sock"* on one leg (C) and a *"stocking"* on the other leg (D). Color the hoof in black (with some blue), and the top part of each leg (above the white markings), with a nice colorful brown.

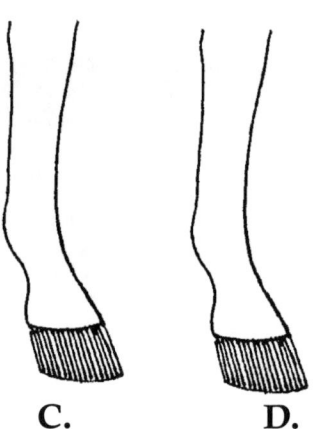

C.   D.

Notice the delightful horse by Haley below, which we repeated four times. The only thing missing is some markings. See if you can give each of the four horses different leg markings. Color your horses with your colored pencils when finished. Finally, give each of your horses a name on the lines below.

"Horse(s)" by Haley Dough Age 12

My name is:

_____ _____ _____ _____

Lesson #23: *Face Markings*

"Horse" by Deseret Scot Age 14 1/2

Many horses have *"markings"* on their faces. Markings not only help distinguish them from other horses, but also can lead to giving them their names. Some of the unique markings found on a horse's face are: a *"snip,"* which is any white marking in between the eyes or on the face (A), a *star,"* which is a white marking on the forehead much like the *snip* but larger (B), a *"stripe,"* which is a narrow white marking that goes down the face (C), a *"blaze,"* which is a large stripe down the nose (D), or a *"freckled"* stripe, which is a stripe speckled with splotches of the horse's natural color (E).

Notice the delightful horse by Deseret above. Do you know the marking on her horse? For this assignment, give each of the horses below a different marking on their face, and then color them in with your colored pencils

A.   B.   C.   D.   E.

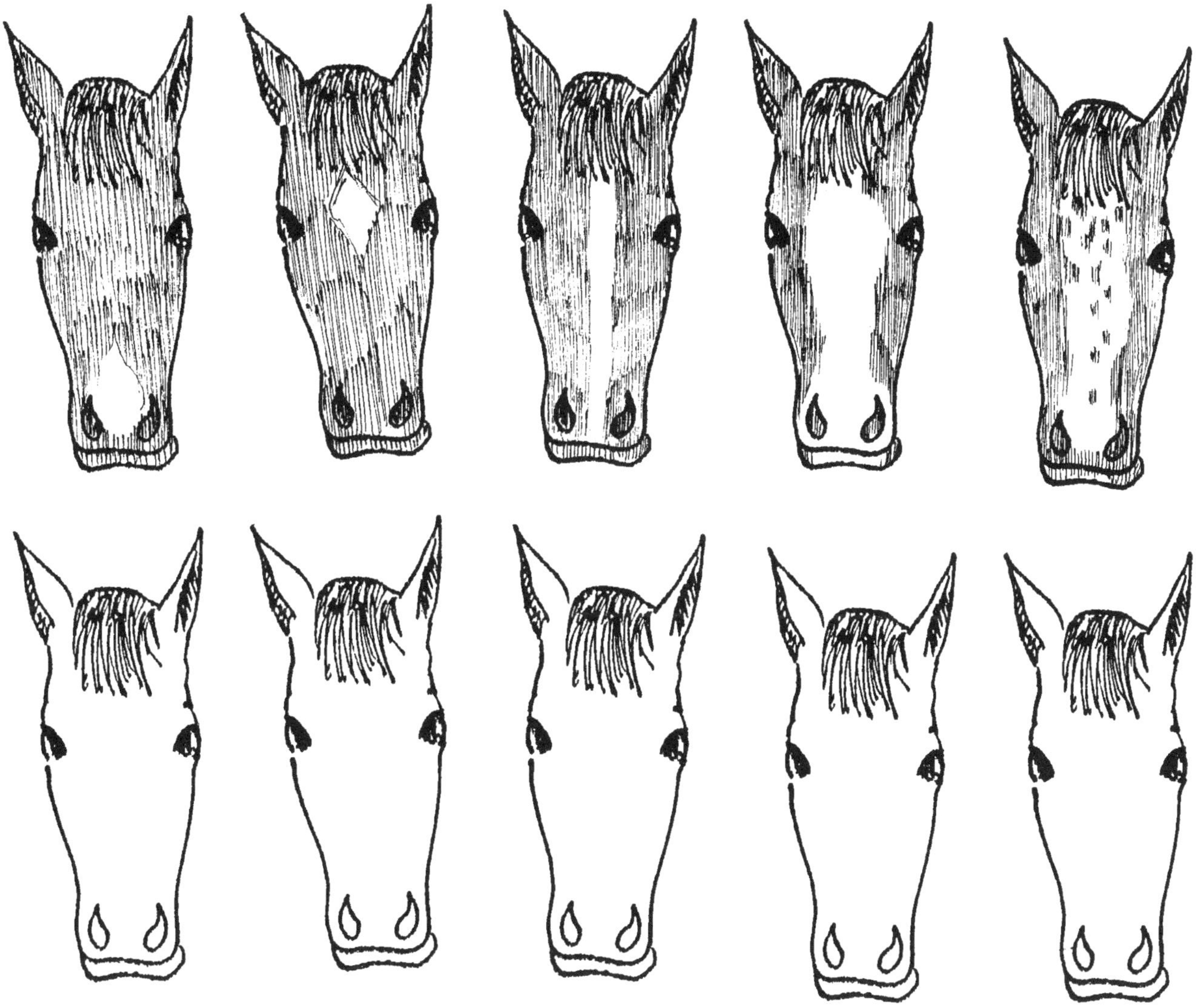

"Let the royal apparel be brought which the king useth to wear, and the horse that the king rideth upon, and the crown which is set upon his head." Exodus 6:8

Lesson #24: *A Saddle Goes Around*

Let's return to the horse we drew in Lesson #7 and complete his body one more time. However, this time put a saddle on him. Since a horse's body is *round* the saddle will also go *around* his body. A saddle is also placed between the two humps of the horse's back. As you know, the front hump is called his *shoulder*, and the back hump is called the *croup*. The saddle will go atop the oval and between the two circles, or humps, as Lily and Molly have so wonderfully illustrated (A & B). First, lightly complete the horse in the figure box below (C), and then draw the saddle going over his back with your yellow colored pencil. When finished, color your horse and saddle with your colored pencils.

A.

"Horse Study" by Lily Davis Age 9

B.

"Horse & Saddle" by Molly Trapp Age 13

C.

"Behold, we put bits in the horses' mouths, that they may obey us; and we turn about their whole body."

James 3:3

Lesson #25: *Bits & Pieces*

A.

In the previous lesson we learned how to draw a saddle on a horse, showing that it goes *around*. Today, let's draw the *bridle* going around the horse's head. The bridle includes: the *browband*, the *noseband*, the *throatlatch*, and the *bit* (A).

A horse has been illustrated for you below, looking in both directions - to the right (B) and to the left (C). Draw the bridle for each horse, going *around* the head; including the browband, noseband, throatlatch, and bit.

Start your drawings lightly with your *HB* pencil and then go over your drawing with your black drawing pen. Finally, print the four parts of the bridle on the lines provided. When you are finished, draw the entire horse's head and bridle, looking both to the right and left in the bottom picture frames (D & E). Color them when finished with your colored pencils, making one a *Chestnut* and the other a *Gray*.

B.

C.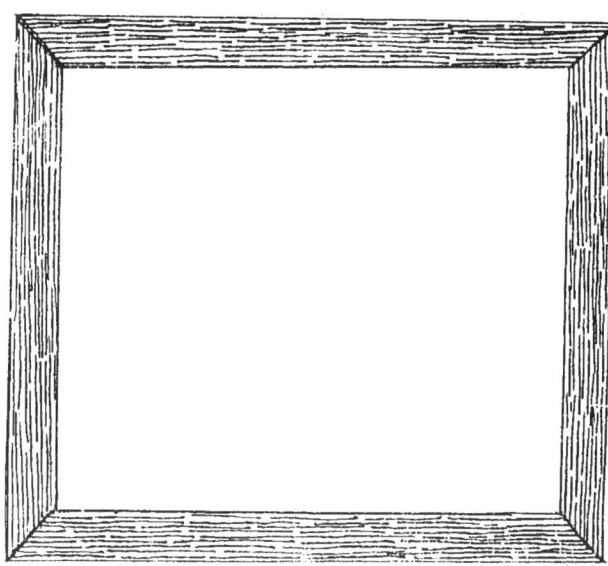

D. Draw Horse's Head & Bridle Here

E.

The Student Gallery

Notice the student drawings to the left and right. The horses are well drawn and the bridle is suggested quite nicely on each. However, both Sarah and Katie could have drawn the bridle going more *around* the head as illustrated in the previous lesson. A horse's head is round.

"Horse's Head" by Sarah Age 10

"Horse's Head" by Katie Stevens Age 16

Lesson #26: *Saddle & Bridle*

Now let's draw a saddle and bridle on a horse in the picture frame below. If you like, you can tie your horse to a stake or fence post, just as Austin did in his drawing (A). Remember, the saddle goes *around* (B) and the bridle goes *around*. Start your drawing lightly with your *HB* pencil and then go over it with your *6B* pencil.

A.

B. A Saddle Goes *"Around"*

"Tied Horse" Austin Lewis Age 9

Horse Sense: Put a scrap piece of paper under your palm to prevent your drawings from smearing.

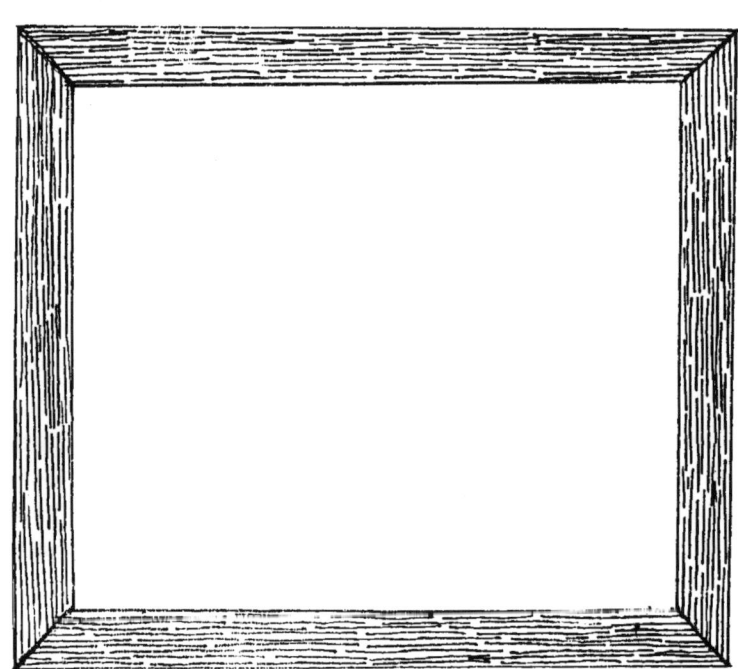

36

Lesson #27: *Horses Walking & Running*

A.

Most beginning students draw horses standing because this is the easiest way to draw a horse. Most also only draw only two legs, again, because this is easiest. For example, take a look at the student drawing to the left. It is a delightful drawing and I like the way Molly drew her horse. But notice that it is standing still and only two legs are showing.

"A Horse" by Molly Trapp Age 13

For today, we are not only going to draw all four legs, but also draw a horse in motion: walking and running. First, copy the legs the way I have illustrated them for you (B) by drawing a line for each part of the legs (C). Then, go around these lines to show the flesh and muscle. Draw all four legs on the last horse. First draw your legs lightly with your yellow pencil, starting with the lines as shown (C). Then, draw the flesh around the lines. When you have finished, go over each with your black drawing pen.

B. Horse Walking   C.

Now let's draw a horse running, which is more difficult than walking. Remember, it takes practice. (If you become frustrated, return to this drawing at a later time. All of us become frustrated with our artwork from time to time.) For a running horse, the body and legs are elongated as the muscles are stretched out more. The tail is also flying in the wind, almost straight behind the horse. First, draw the legs on the running horse. To begin, draw the simple lines showing the correct angles of each leg, and then draw around these lines to show the shapes of the legs and hooves (D). Finally, draw the entire horse in the figure box with its tail blowing in the wind.

D. Horse Running

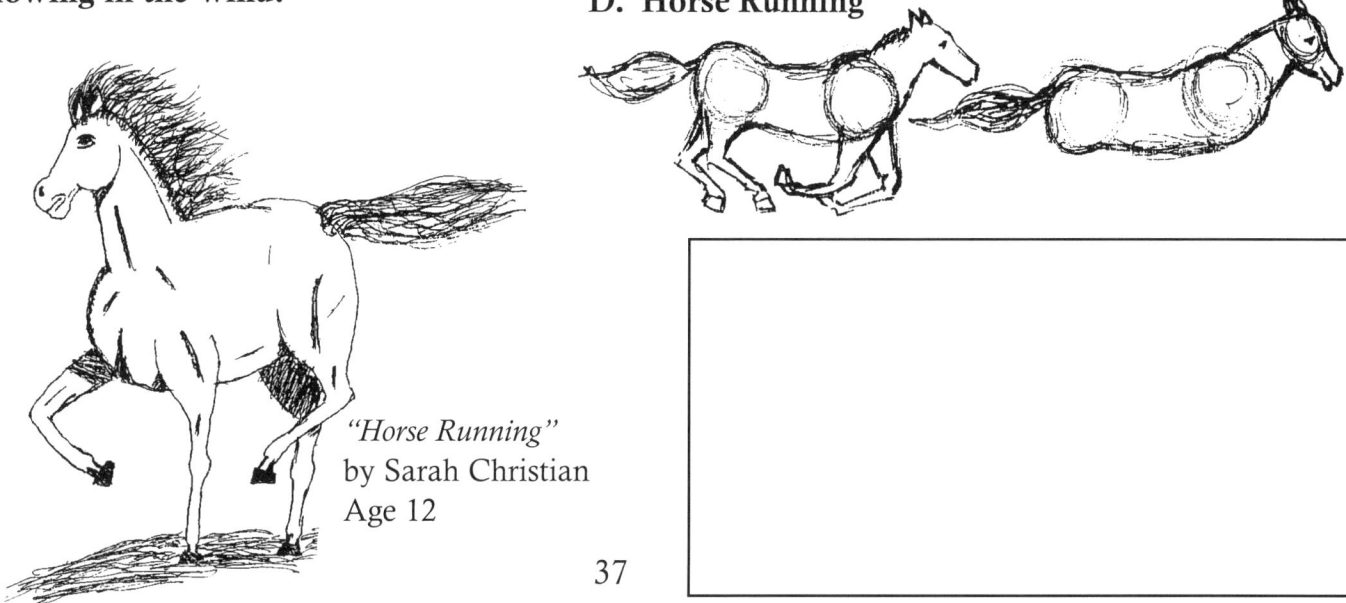

"Horse Running" by Sarah Christian Age 12

Lesson #28: *"Blowing in the Wind"*

In the last lesson, we practiced drawing a running horse. This is not easy to do because it is difficult to draw the legs at different angles. Notice the horse by Kayla below (A). She did a wonderful job but had a little problem with the movements of the legs. Also, notice Alex's delightful running horse (B). It looks like he certainly enjoys drawing horses!

A.

B.

"A Horse" by Kayla Prusaitis Age 10

"Running Horse" by Alan Perry Age 6

When a horse is running, all the legs are at different angles. (Turn to page 45 and look at the pictures of Muybridge's running horse and the different angles of the legs.) Remember, when a horse is running the muscles are stretched and the legs seem longer and thinner. As in the last exercise, draw the top part of your horse first (C), then the angle of each leg with lines (D). Go over the lines for the legs by adding muscle and flesh, drawing the mane and tail blowing in the wind (E). Draw a running horse in the picture frame below with your colored pencils.

C.   D. 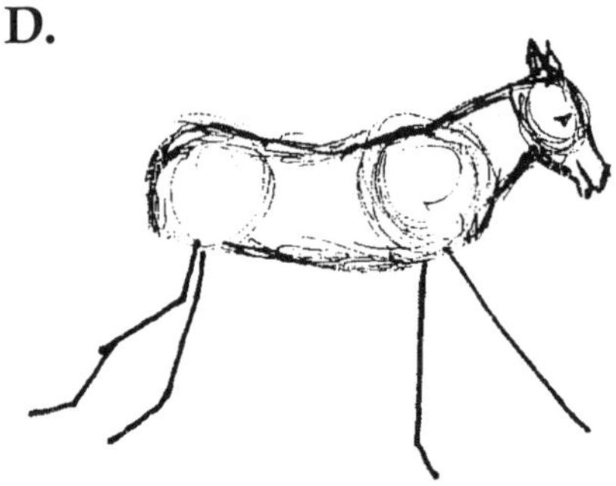   E.

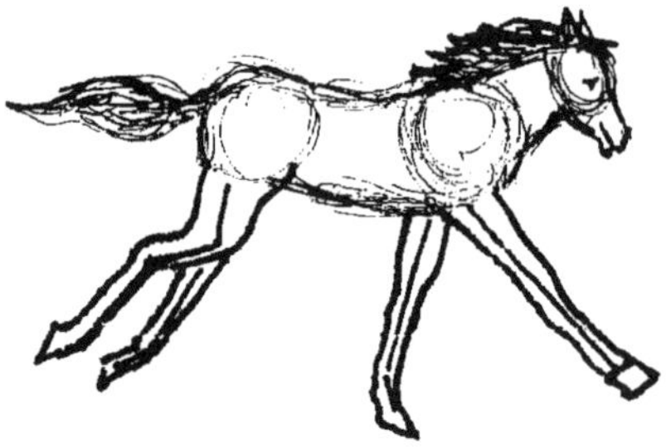

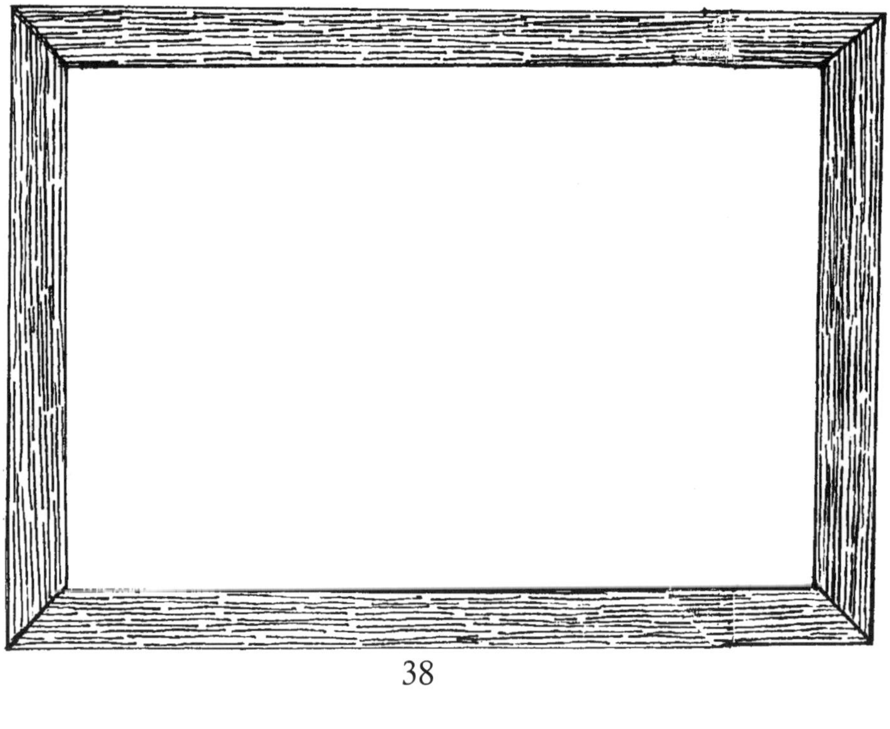

Lesson #29: *Ride'm Cowboy!*

Now that you have drawn a horse and a saddle, let's draw a cowboy! Do you know how to draw the human figure? You may want to start by drawing *"hot dog"* figures. To do this, first draw a stick figure in the position you desire for your person (A). Then add long, thin hot dog shapes for the arms, legs, and body; an oval shape for the head; and small round circles for the hands (B). Finally, put some clothes and a hat on your cowboy and he is ready to say, *"Gid-e-e-e-up!"* (C). Draw your horse and cowboy in the figure box below (D) with your colored pencils.

"Howdy" Daniel Margulis Age 7

A.

B.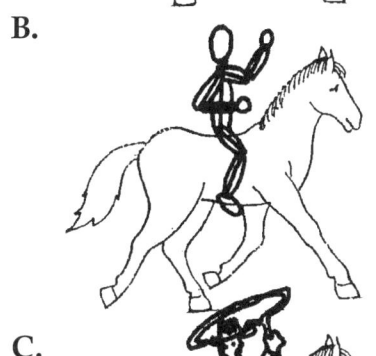

C.

D. Draw Your Horse and Cowboy Here

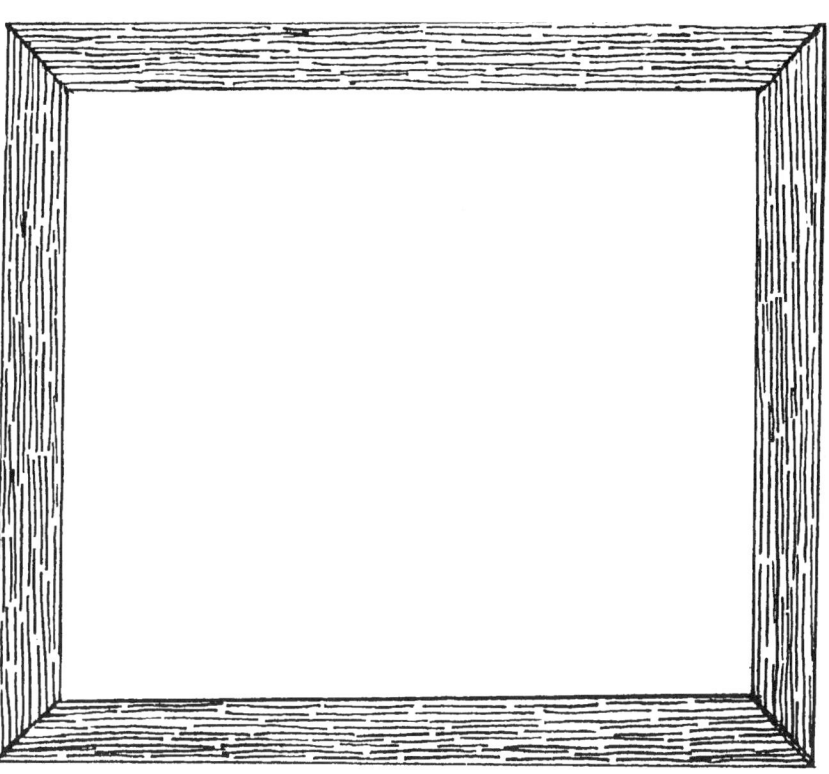

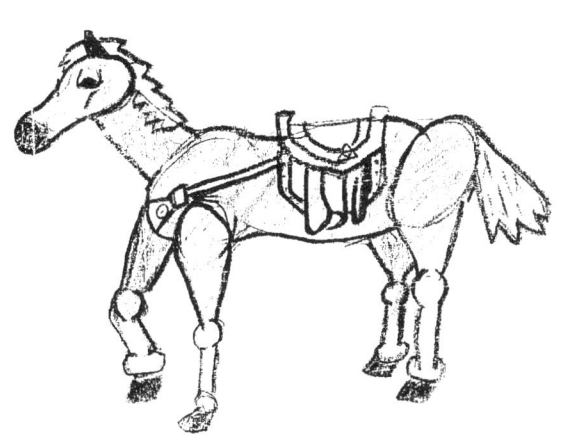

"Horse & Saddle" Jarrett Moore Age 13

"Horse & Cowboy" by David Margulis Age 12

Lesson #30: *Corralling a Horse*

For this lesson, we are going to *overlap*, which means placing one object in front of another to show *depth* in your picture. As an example, let's place Alex Dib's horse (A) inside a fence. First, draw the horse with your yellow colored pencil in the large figure box below. Corral your horse by placing a fence in front of him as we did below. Draw your fence posts lightly with your orange colored pencil, making sure the posts are evenly spaced and the same height as shown (B). Then, draw two, long pieces of wood going into each post. See if you can make your lines straight, but do not use a ruler. This is called practicing *control* with your pencil. When you have the fence drawn in front of your horse, color it with your orange, violet and brown pencils; using long, broken lines to show *texture* in the wood. Finally, darken the parts of your horse that you can see behind the fence with your black colored pencil (C). Do you want to add anything else to your picture, like a red barn in the distance or some flowers in the foreground?

A. B. C.

"Horse" by Alex Dib Age 9

Horse Sense
Draw lightly and then go over everything with a darker pencil.

Lesson #31: *Horses in the Pasture*

Let's now draw three horses in a pasture. Draw one in the *foreground*, one in the *middleground*, and one in the *background*. Objects which are in the foreground are not only larger but also have more detail. Whereas, objects in the background are smallest and have little detail. Therefore, the horse in the middleground will be larger than the horse in the background but smaller than the horse in the foreground (A), as shown with the delightful horse by Brittany Townsend. Also, when drawing several horses, you may want to draw them in different directions - looking to the left or looking to the right. Draw your picture with a light colored pencil and then color it in using a lot of creative colors. Can you make a colorful red for your barn, having a light side and a shaded side? For the light side you may want to use yellow, orange, and red. For the shaded side, try adding some blue or violet to your red to make it darker. In the opened barn door use violet, blue, and a little red to make a dark color. Practice coloring your barn with the two barns below (B). Finally, complete your drawing in the figure box on the bottom of the page.

A. background   B.

"Horse" by Brittany Townsend Age 11

Lesson #32: *Now You See It - Now You Don't*

Can you *camouflage* a horse so that it blends in with its surroundings? For example, look at the two excellent student drawings of horses below and notice that they are somewhat camouflaged. For this assignment, draw a horse in the figure box below having it blend in with its surroundings. You may want to use rocks and boulders, a brown or tan desert, woodlands, or anything else you can imagine! Try to conceal your horse so well that it is difficult to see! When finished, color it in with your colored pencils making sure to use the same colors in the horse as in its surroundings.

Drawing by Marta Stolen Age 10   Drawing by Kate Whiting Age 10

Lesson #33:
Drawing the Horse's Head - Front View

"A Horse" by Emrie Prather

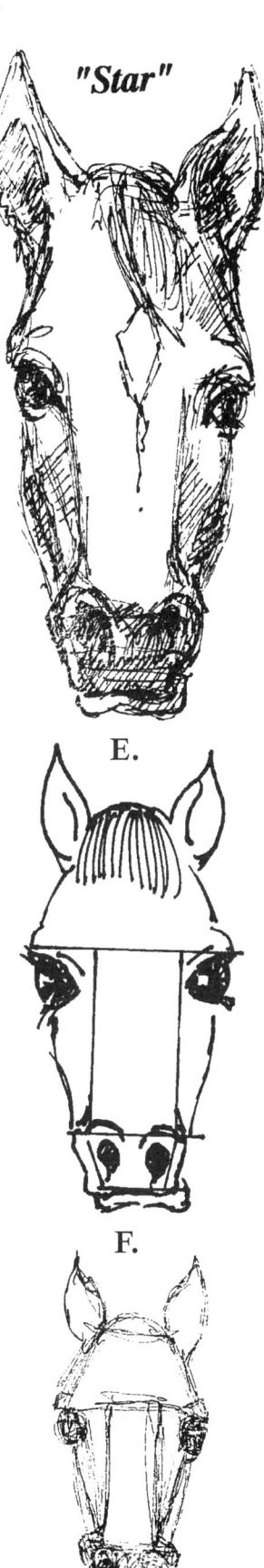

"Star"

Let's draw the front view of a horse's head by using more geometric shapes. First, draw a trapezoid for the forehead (A). Add to this a fairly long rectangle (B). At the bottom of the rectangle draw a smaller trapezoid for the nose (C). A horse's eyes are nearly on the side of his head, giving him the ability to see to both sides and partially to the rear. Draw a round circle for each eye where the forehead meets with the rectangle (D). Round out the top of the horse's head and draw two leaf shapes for the ears. Then draw the *forelock* (the part of the mane that comes out over the forehead). For the nostrils, draw two upside-down teardrop shapes and add a bottom lip, drawing it a little to one side (E).

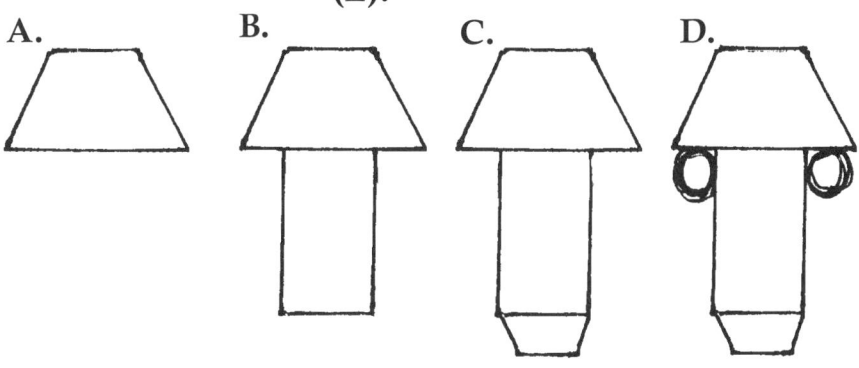

A horse has long muscles on the sides of his head. So, last of all, draw these muscles curving along the side of his jaws up to his eyes (F). Finally, soften the lines so that they are not too angular, as in the portrait of *"Star"* above.

Do your drawing of the horse's head in the figure box. Start with your yellow colored pencil. When you have everything drawn correctly, go over it with your darker colored pencils.

43

"I will not follow where the path may lead, but I will go where there is no path, and I will leave a trail."

Muriel Strode

Lesson #34: *Horses, Horses Everywhere*

"Lipizzan Colt"
by Juliana Jordan
Age 11

Let's now draw horses everywhere! For this lesson, draw a horse standing on grass in the sunshine (A). A horse in the city (B). A horse on a farm (C). A horse running with mountains in the background (D). Can you put lots of detail in your pictures? Use your imagination and be creative! Try to draw each horse in a different position: one looking right, one looking left, one walking, and one running. Make sure to color in your pictures when finished, using lots of colorful colors.

A. Horse Standing on Grass in Sunshine

B. Horse in the City

C. Horse on a Farm

D. Horse Running with Mountains in Background

Lesson #35: *Flip Book - Horse in Action!*

Eadweard Muybridge (1830-1904) was an English-American photographer. He was also one of the earliest known photographers. One of the things he studied was living creatures, both men and animals. He would photograph different sequels of men and animals in action to show how their various parts moved. You could say this was the beginning of motion pictures. Muybridge was able to demonstrate through his photographs that all four legs of a running horse are off the ground at the same time. One book he wrote was titled, *"Horse in Motion."* Look at the photographs by Muybridge of a horse in motion below (D). This is a great study for any student of horses to see the various movements of a running horse.

Let's now see if you can put a horse in action on paper. Have you ever heard of a *flip book*? It is simply a collection of small pages that are stapled together with an illustration drawn on each. When the book is flipped through it will create animated action.

First, take the small illustrations of the horse on the next page and make several copies. (Use a sturdy, cover stock paper for your copies, which can easily be done at any office supply store). Then, carefully cut out each frame going around the outlines of the figure boxes. Place them together in a neat stack, rotating the horse in one position (A) with the other position on the next page (B). Continue this until you finish your booklet and then staple the top part of your flip book together with two staples (C). Finally, using your thumb, flip through your book and watch your horse run across the pages (E)!

A.

B.

C.

D. Muybridge's Horse in Motion

E.

Lesson #36: *Cartooning*

"Cartooning" is a style of art that is more simple and comical than *"realistic"* art. In cartooning the features are both simplified and exaggerated. For example, look at the horse drawing in Lesson #7 that you completed. He is certainly more *cartoony* than *realistic*. Notice how the eyes were drawn large and egged-shaped. Does that look like a horse's eyes? In cartooning you have the liberty to change and exaggerate the features to make your character look more comical.

"A Horse" by Davis Clark Age 10

Some students, especially younger ones, have a tendency to naturally make their horses more cartoony because their drawings are more simplified (as illustrated in Davis' delightful drawing above). Other students who like to cartoon, incorporate this into a more sophisticated style, as shown in some of the student examples on the next page.

For this assignment, complete the horses' heads below by adding facial features to each. You can use any of the eyes, noses, mouths, and ears provided, or be creative and make your own. First, return to Lesson #33 and draw the basic structure of the horses heads in the ovals. Then, lightly draw the cartoon features in with your *HB* pencil. Go over each head with your black drawing pen when finished.

Cartoon Facial Features

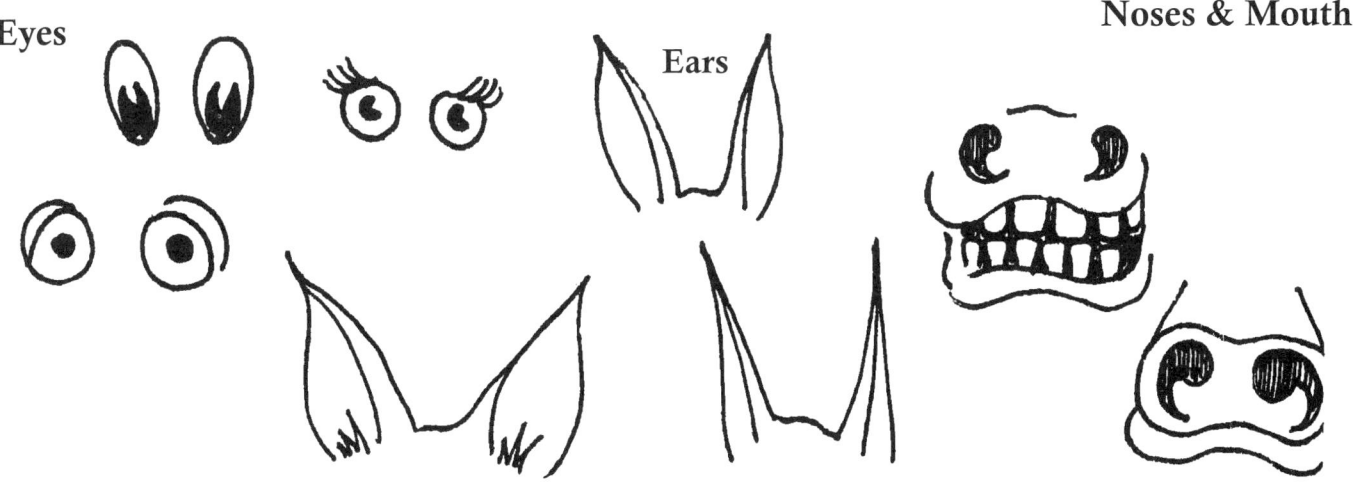

Complete the Horse's Heads Below

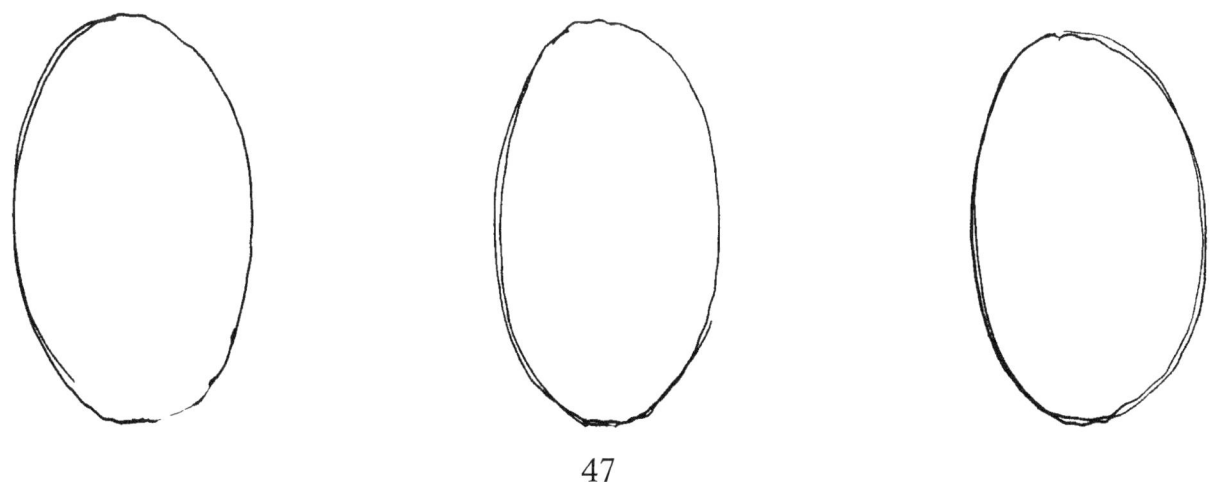

"A Horse" by Kelsey Moore Age 9

"Horse Drawing" by Andrew Noordermeer Age 12

Artwork by Aaron Christian Age 14

Artwork by Emily Turk Age 7

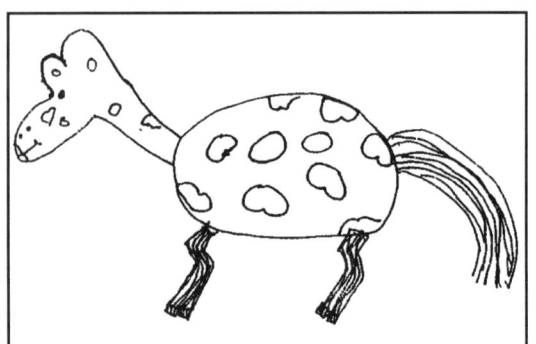

Artwork by Carina Botterbusch Age 10

My Horse by _____

Lesson #37: *A Mazing Horse*

Let's imagine your horse has strayed away from home. He is not in the pasture because he broke through the fence, and now your horse is trying to find his way home (observe the delightful drawing by Anna below). For this assignment, draw a maze for your horse to go through, making many paths but only one leading to home. You can put hurdles in the way to block certain paths, such as a *"highway," "mountain," "river"* (A), or any other obstacle you like. You can make winding paths (B) or straight ones by using a ruler (C). Can you draw your horse at the beginning of the maze (D)?

"A Horse" by Anna Brinkman Age 11

Draw your maze with your *HB* pencil in your sketchbook, and then go over everything with your black pen when finished. After you have completed your maze, make some copies of it and challenge your friends to see if they can lead your horse home in less than 30 seconds.

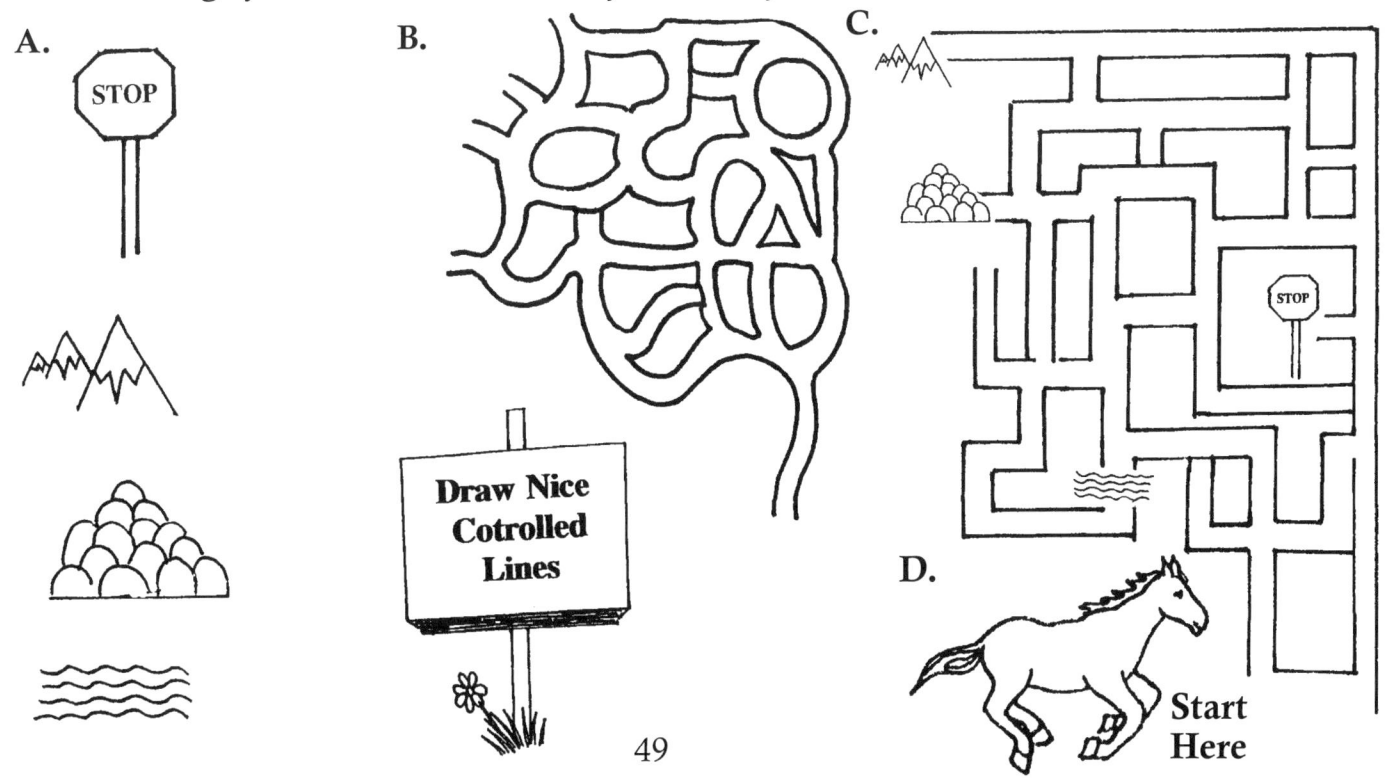

Lesson #38: *"Once Upon a Time there was a Horse..."*

For this assignment, let's write and illustrate a story about a horse in the figure boxes below and on the next page. First, complete the story line which has already been started for you. Then draw your pictures in the figure boxes provided. Start your drawings lightly with your yellow colored pencil, and then go over everything with your other colored pencils.

"Once upon a time there was a horse named _____. He lived during the _____ century, in a land where there were lots of _____ and _____. His owner's name was _____, who was a kind, old man who lived in a _____. One day, while _____ (your horse's name) was running in a field he came across a _____ hiding in the tall grasses!!!

Complete your story here:

_____
_____
_____
_____
_____
_____
_____
_____
_____
_____
_____
_____
_____
_____
_____
_____
_____
_____
_____
_____
_____
_____
_____
_____

Name _____   Date: _____

Lesson #39: Horse Examination #1
(Answers may be found in Part I of text)

1. Put a bridle on the horse's head and label the parts.

2. Color the three horses (below), creating a different color brown for each by mixing your colors.

3. Draw a saddle on the horse's back.

4. Draw a trapezoid.

5. Where is the fetlock on a horse's leg?

6. Draw a parallelogram.

7. Draw a horse using a light source and shade certain parts of it.

8. A horse with large spots is called a _____.

9. A horse with small spots is called a _____.

10. _____ are the building blocks in art.

11. A _____ colored horse can vary from a mouse gray to a sandy color.

12. A _____ is a white part of the leg below the fetlock joint.

Matching

(Match the shape with the part of the body by placing the correct letter of the definition next to the number in the left column)

1. large oval shape   a. thigh & neck
2. parallelogram   b. bottom of leg, *cannon*
3. trapezoid   c. ear
4. long, thin rectangle   d. belly
5. leaf-shape   e. nostril
6. tear drop   f. hoof
7. Palomino   g. a reddish-brown horse
8. star   h. a white marking between the eyes
9. Chestnut   i. a gold colored horse
10. sock   j. a marking on the bottom of the leg

Student Art Gallery

"Mishaah" by Ashley Hollandsworth Age 16

"Horse Study" by Kate Burch Age 12

"Horse Study" by Mark Puder Age 11

Student Art Gallery

"Horse Study" by Joshua Newborn Age 13

The Wonderful Art of
Drawing Horses

Part II
Intermediate Horse Drawing

"Wild Horse" by Noah Sanders Age 13

Lesson #40: *The Anatomy of a Horse*

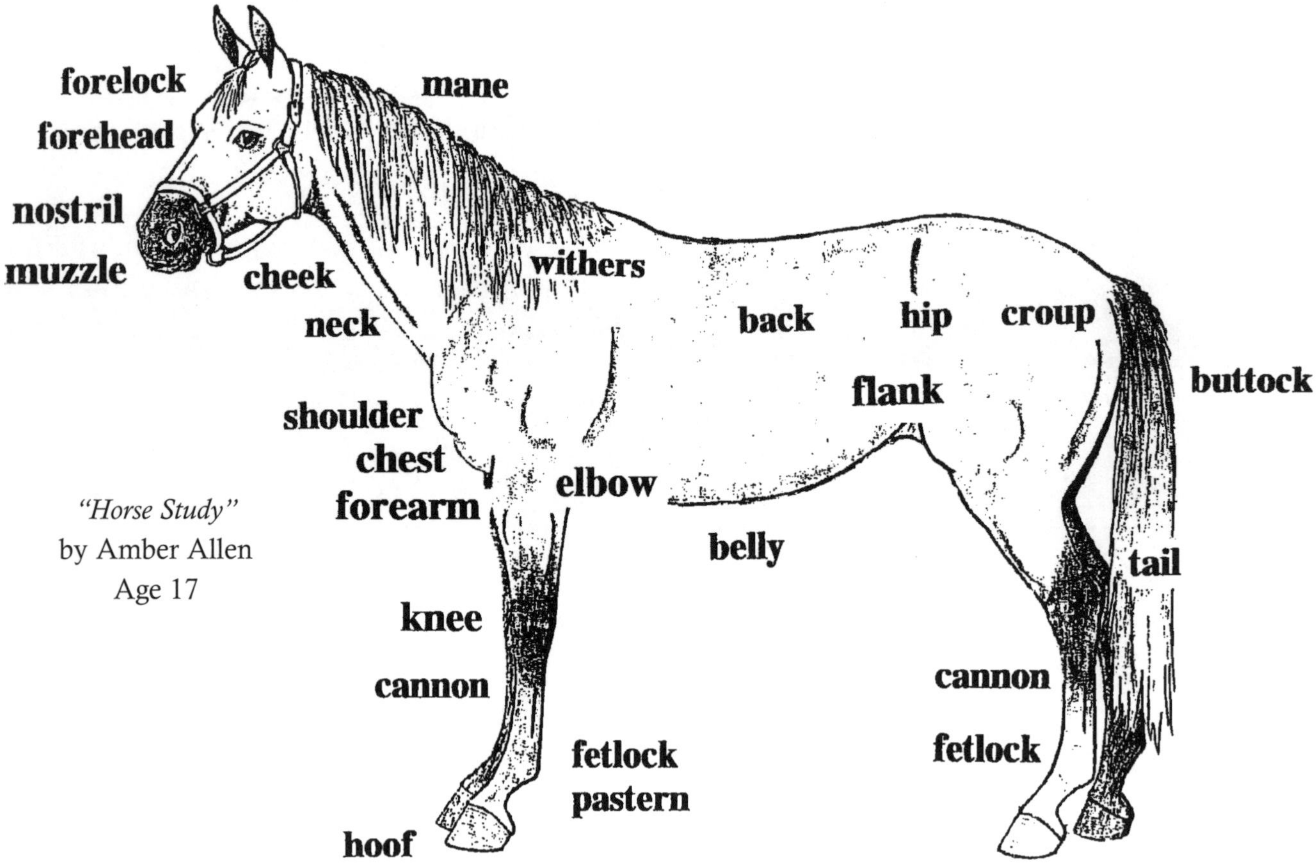

"Horse Study" by Amber Allen Age 17

Above is an excellent illustration of a horse by Amber Allen. As you can see, many of the parts of the horse have been labeled. For this assignment, copy Amber's horse in the figure box below and label the parts. Use your best lettering and draw a straight line with a ruler from the term to the part of the horse. Start your drawing with an *HB* pencil and then go over it with a darker pencil when finished.

Lesson #41: *Learning the Skeleton*

In order to draw something properly, it is almost as important to learn what's inside an object as it is to learn what's on the outside. For example, it would greatly help in drawing a bag of apples to know that apples were inside the bag. Knowing such things will assist in giving your subject matter better form. The same is true with drawing a horse, as learning its skeleton will assist in drawing the horse properly.

For the first part of this exercise, draw the flesh going around the skeleton of the horse below (A). Then label all the parts as shown. Remember the shape of the belly, croup, shoulder, and legs. Finally, see if you can draw the skeleton of a horse in your sketchbook. Then label the parts and draw the flesh going around the skeleton. Use your drawing pencils for this assignment and start your drawing lightly.

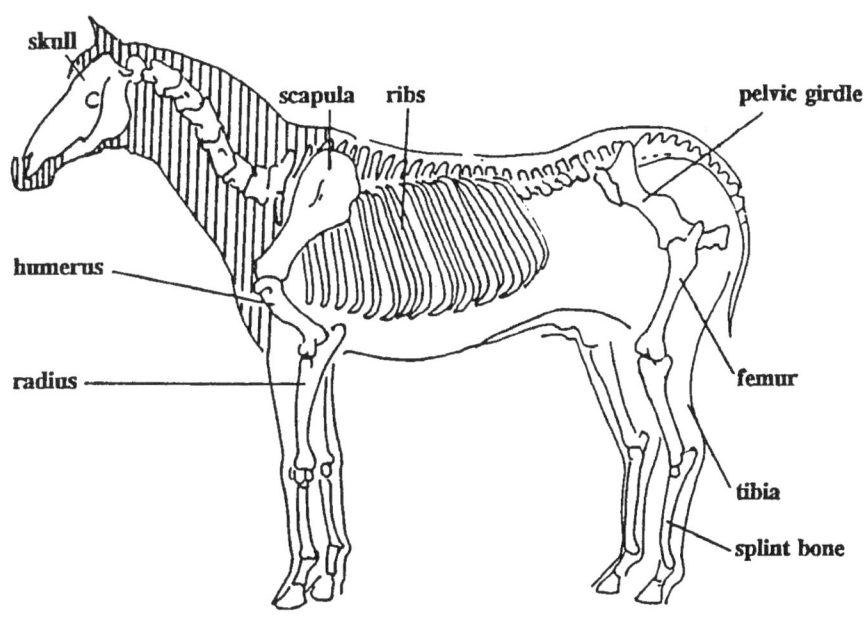

A.

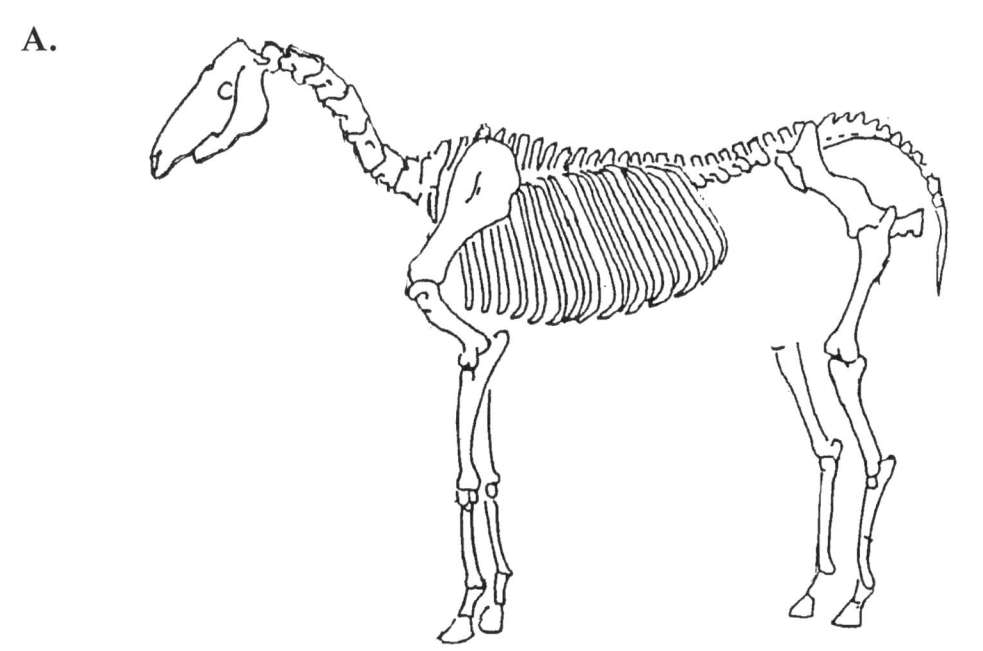

The Definition of a Horse

For this lesson, read the definition of a horse below and answer the questions on the next page:

Websters (hors) n. 1. A four-footed, solid-hoofed animal used for riding or for pulling loads; the male as distinct from a mare or a colt. In zoology, a general name applied to the family of horses, asses, and zebras which belongs to the odd-toed order of hoofed mammals, and is characterized by possessing only a single toe on the foot. A typical horse is distinguished from asses and zebras by having a flowing mane and forelock, smaller ears, and by the tail being longhaired to the root. However, it is in the domesticated races of horses that the differences in the mane and tail are most obvious; for in the single existing wild species, the mane is *hogged* and the tail scantily hairy at the root. The earliest records of the horse as a domesticated animal suggest that it was used mainly in warfare, or for riding or drawing a chariot. For these purposes a combination of speed, endurance, and strength were required. There were many breeds of horses that were used to create other horses for different purposes, however, the horses that most greatly influenced the modern European horses were the Barb and Arab, both of which came from North Africa and were famous for speed and hardiness.

Domesticated horses, like most domesticated animals, show every gradation in color from black, through Bay, Chestnut, Dun, to gray, and white, (or a combination of these tints). Although there were no horses in America when it was first discovered, the evidence of fossil remains shows that horses were, at one time, found all over North America. The horses in North America eventually died off after most had traveled and relocated to Asia and Europe by northern routes when the continents were connected. The intelligence of a horse is much less than that of a dog, but it is extremely docile and responds to kind treatment. During its roaming existence the horse would live on grass and other wild *"cereals,"* which provided all the nutrition it needed. However, energy-producing foods such as oats, corn, barley, leguminous plants and the like are necessary for a working horse. Horses should be fed at least four times a day. When feeding a horse precaution must be taken against either overloading the stomach or allowing it to remain empty too long. Chopped hay is often mixed with the corn to prevent *"bolting."* Oats are the usual food for horses, up to 10 lbs per day, together with a like quantity of hay. The horse's digestion works rapidly, so that he can work continuously with short rests. Horses can sleep standing up, but a soft bed is provided in the stable, which should be kept clean. Male horses are usually castrated in this country when the foal is a year old; a castrated animal is called a *"gelding."* A mare casts her foal from 345 to 365 days after conception. The most troublesome ailment of horses is colic, caused by the retention of gases in the belly from fermentation of food, and often brought on by a change in feeding habits.

"Horse"
by Jonathan Puder
Age 9

"A Horse"
by Stacy Roberson Age 12

Lesson #42:

Answer the following questions:

1. Horses were mainly used for two purposes. What were they?
_____
_____

2. What is the unique characteristic of a horse's foot?
_____
_____

3. What three things distinguish the horse from asses and zebras?

1._____

2._____

3._____

4. What were the three main qualities, or traits, in a horse that were most desired?

1._____

2._____

3._____

Fill in the Blanks:

1. The horses that most influenced the modern European horses were the _____ and the _____ which came from _____ _____.
2. Domesticated horses have many different gradations of color such as _____, _____, _____, _____, _____, and _____ .
3. The intelligence of a horse is much less than that of a _____ .
4. Horses are extremely docile and respond to _____ _____.
5. In the wild, horses would eat _____ and other wild _____.
6. Contemporary working horses need foods like _____, _____, _____, and _____.
7. Oats are the usual food for horses and they require up to _____ pounds per day.
8. A mare casts her foal from _____ to _____ days after conception.

Three Ways to Draw a Horse

There are three ways to draw a horse: copying from a picture, drawing from memory, or drawing from life. Many young students draw horses from memory. As students grow older, they tend to want to make a more realistic horse so they copy from pictures. Both of these approaches are much easier than drawing a horse from life. Not many students attempt drawing live horses because it can be very frustrating as horses will move on you! However, if you plan to be a serious student of drawing horses, it is recommended you also learn to draw them from life. No picture can take the place of the actual thing. With pencil and sketchbook in hand, you can have these large, strong, beautiful creatures before your very eyes with all the wonderful details. Drawing from life will teach you to see - to observe horses and how God has constructed them from the hooves, to the mane, to the muscles, to the features of the head.

Three Ways to Draw A Horse:
1. Copy from Pictures
2. Draw from Imagination
3. Draw from Life Studies or Statues

As mentioned, drawing from *"life"* can be frustrating because, most of the time, horses will not stand still. Here are some pointers that may help you get started. For one, learn to work quickly copying down just the essentials. This is called quick *"gesture drawings."* Stay away from all the details and see if you can copy the most essential parts of the horse. For example, you do not have to concern yourself with the facial features, or all the details in the legs and muscles. Notice the quick study of horses below, which was done in a few minutes. As you can see, many of the strokes were very quick and there is little suggestion of detail. Remember, gesture drawing is not easy. You literally have to do hundreds of such sketches before you will be satisfied. Just do not give up. It can be a wonderful course for studying horses!

"Quick Study of Horses in Lone Pine, California" by Barry Stebbing

Lesson #43: *Copying from a Picture*

As mentioned, copying from a picture is the easiest way to draw a horse. This is because the horse will not move. In the beginning, it is probably best to copy horses from drawings, pictures, or photographs. However, as one learns more about horses, the student should also practice drawing horses using other approaches. The one concern about copying from pictures is that the drawings tend to be *"flat,"* not showing much structure or form. That is why drawing from life, or sculpted models, is beneficial, as it will help you to structure the horse with three dimensional form.

Turn to the drawing on the next page that I did of a horse copied from a picture. This drawing was done in pencil and was enjoyable to do. Since I have done many studies from life, I was able to give the horse more form. One way of showing form is with the use of shading to show that parts of the body go around. For this assignment, find a picture of a horse in a book or magazine and draw it in the figure box below with your drawing pencils. Start off lightly with you *HB* pencil and then go to a darker drawing pencil, shading some areas to show form. Be aware of the *"negative space"* when drawing. This is the space in between parts of your subject matter. For example, study the *negative space* between the head and the neck (A) and also between the legs (B). When you are finished, write how you feel about your drawing on the lines at the bottom of the next page, stating what you like and dislike about drawing from a picture.

A. Negative Space

B. Negative Space

Lesson #44: *Copying A Horse* For this assignment, copy the drawing of a horse below. Using your drawing pencils, draw your horse on a sheet of white paper or in your sketchbook. Remember to see the negative space as mentioned in the previous lesson. Finish your drawing with your darkest drawing pencil.

Lesson #45: *More Pictures to Copy From*

Find some more photos of horses to copy in the figure boxes below. Start your drawings off lightly, making sure to see the *negative space* in between the parts of each horse (as between the legs and under the neck). Also, try to shade some parts of the body like the shoulder, legs, flank, or croup to show form. Use your colored pencils and place your horses in nice surroundings.

Lesson #46: *Facial Features \ Side View Part II*

In Lesson #16 we learned how to draw the facial features of a horse. Let's take this a step further, learning more about drawing these features. As mentioned, the ears are shaped like a leaf from the front view and the fin of a porpoise from the side view (A). However, a horse's ear has more poetic lines than just a simple leaf or fin shape and should have nice curves and form.

Likewise, the eye in profile is more than simply a bird-shape with a circle in it (B). As you develop your skills you will notice that a horse's eye is a large sphere covered by a heavy eye-lid going *around* it. The pupil of the eye is darkest and the iris (the larger part of the circle) can be drawn with wagon wheel spokes that go around the pupil. Do not forget to leave a sparkle, or highlight, in your eyes.

Remember, the nose is first drawn with a fairly large oval, and the end of the nose is drawn at a slant (C). This area of the horse's head is usually of a darker value and should be shaded. Copy the horse's head shown in the figure box (D), applying these basic pointers when drawing the ears, eyes, and nose. Draw your horse's head in the picture frame below with your *HB* pencil and go over it with your *5B* pencil when finished.

"A Horse"
by Kate Woronowicz Age 11

Lesson #47: *Front View - Drawing a Horse's Head Part II*

We have practiced drawing the head of a horse in previous lessons. For this assignment, let's draw it again, learning more about the proper structure. First, instead of a trapezoid (as done in Lesson #33), draw a circle for the forehead and then add the long oval for the nose (A). Next, square off the nose by drawing a long rectangle inside the oval from the top to bottom (B). The eyes of a horse are round so draw a round circle on the outside of the larger circle (forehead), and just to the left and right of the top of the rectangle (C). The nose is drawn with a trapezoid to show its wedge-shape, the nostrils are upside down tear drops, and this entire part of the nose is shaded (D). The ears have a curved, leaf shape, however, there is a darker value inside each ear. A thin, long muscle extends down the sides of the head from the eye to the nose (E). Finally, sketch in the forelock (front of the mane) and suggest the shoulders (F). Draw your horse's head in the figure box on the bottom of the page with your drawing pencils.

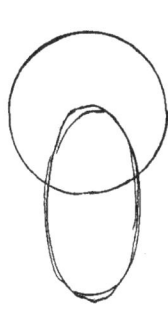 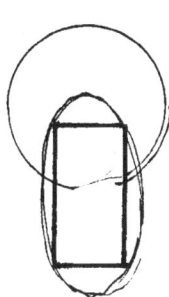 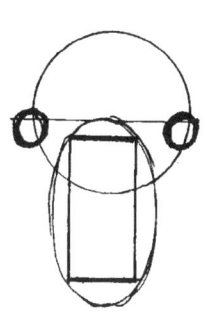 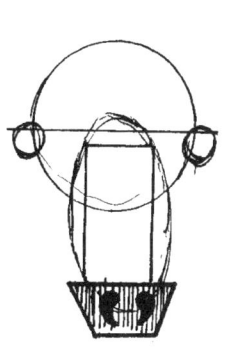 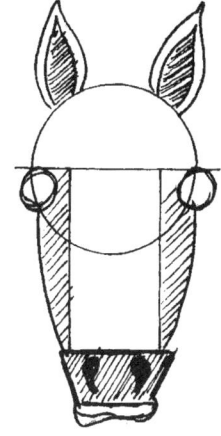

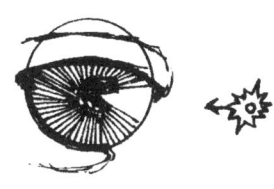

Note: Remember, the eye is a large circle with the eyelid going around it. An easy way to make the eye is to draw a small circle in the middle for the pupil and leave a pie shape for the highlight. For the iris, (the larger circle that goes around the pupil) simply use wheel spokes going around the iris close together. Make sure to leave a pie shape for the highlight in the iris also.

F.

"A Horse"
by John Moist Age 6

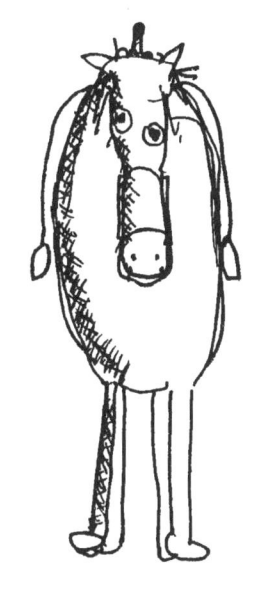

Lesson #48: *Front View*

There are basically three positions in which a horse is drawn: *front view*, *side view*, and *rear view*. The *side view* being the most popular with students, quite possibly because this view shows the true majesty of a horse (A).

A. Side View

"A Horse" by Kirsten Bailey Age 9

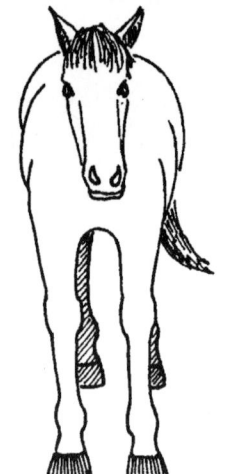

Today we are going to learn how to draw the *front view* (B). This is the position you see when standing in front of a horse. When drawing a horse in this position, you should be aware of *overlapping,* placing one part slightly in front of another (C). Overlapping is necessary in order to put the head in front of the neck, the neck in front of the shoulders, the shoulders in front of the belly, the belly in front of the rump, the rump in front of the tail, and the forelegs in front of the rear legs.

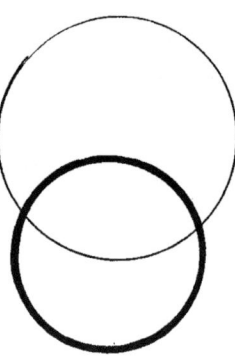

C. Overlapping

B. Front View

"Horse Study" by Stephen Coffey Age 10

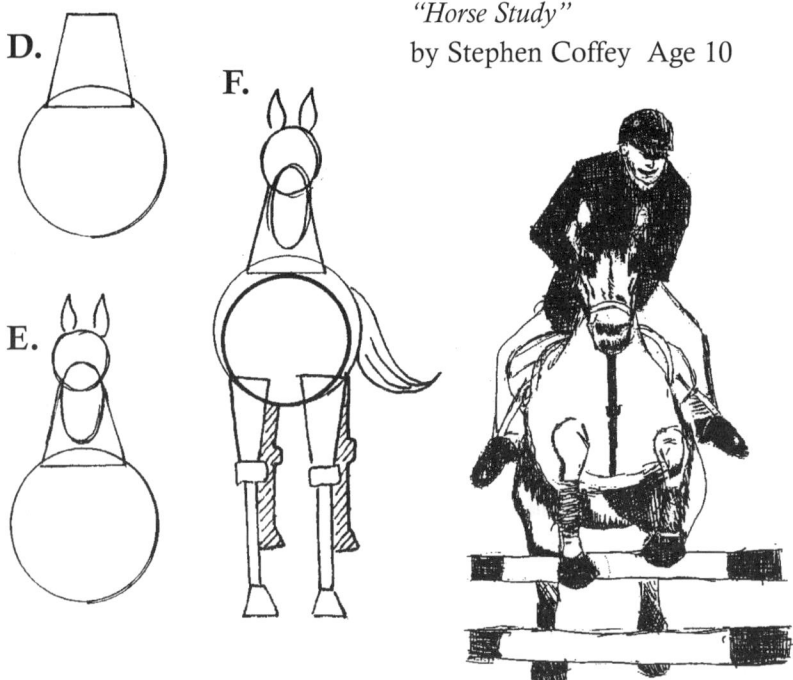

First, using your yellow pencil, draw a fairly large circle for the horse's shoulders. Then draw the trapezoid shape for his neck (D), and draw his head and nose over the trapezoid (E). For the belly, lightly draw a smaller circle, overlapping the circle for the shoulders. Draw the front legs and then the rear legs, and suggest the tail behind the horse (F). (Remember, the rear legs will be higher up on the paper.) When finished, use your brown colored pencil to go over the parts of the horse you will see from this view. Finally, smooth out and add details to your horse with your black pencil. Draw the front view of your horse in the figure box above.

Lesson #49: *Rear View*

The rear view is probably the most difficult to draw, simply because it doesn't seem to *look right* when we draw it. There is less *overlapping* with this view than with the front view, and less attention to the neck and head as the rump of the horse takes pre-eminence.

Starting with your yellow colored pencil, draw the rear view of a horse in the figure box below. First draw a large circle for the rump of your horse which is now going to be closest to you. Then, do as you did in the previous lesson by overlapping the circles for the shoulders (A). You can add the neck and head in this position, making sure to draw them smaller since they are more distant. Draw the rear legs first, which are closest to you, and a curved line that equally divides the rump in half (B). (Make this line light because a dark line on a horse in this area is considered a *dorsal stripe*). Next, draw the forelegs, which need to be a little shorter, and the tail of your horse (C).

When you are finished, go over your drawing with your black colored pencil, smoothing out many of the lines and only going over what is showing. The rear view of a horse may not be too exciting to you, but it can be a good angle to use in a field behind your feature horse or other horses. With the rear view you can either draw the horse's head above his body, show him grazing, or simply leave the head out (D).

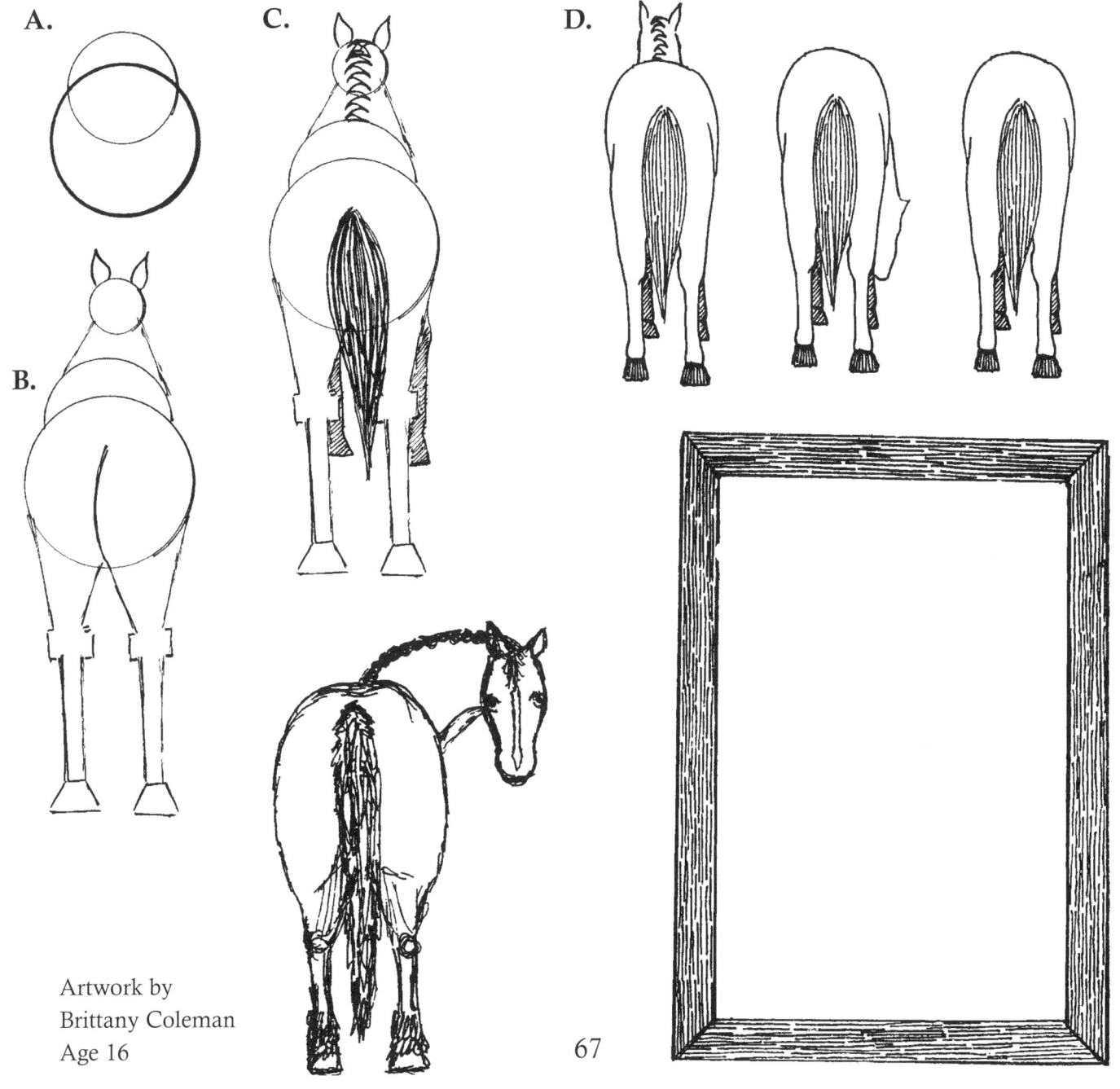

Artwork by
Brittany Coleman
Age 16

Lesson #50: *Studying from a Statue*

"Bishop Absalon" 1128-1201

In art academies, one of the first assignments for students is to draw from *"cast objects."* Cast objects can be anything from statues, to monuments, to cast models. The great advantage with such a study is that these objects do not move. This will allow the student to focus on the *light*, various *values* from light to dark, and *form*.

Drawing a horse in such a manner is an excellent study, teaching the student a great deal about the proper *proportions* of body parts along with showing specific features like the muscles or various areas of the head and body.

"Frederik D. Syvende"

While traveling through Europe, I had the opportunity to sketch several monuments. The two horse studies on this page were drawn in the city of Copenhagen. For this assignment, copy the drawing (left) of the statue of *Frederik D. Syvende* in the figure box on the next page.

Start your drawing very lightly with your *HB* drawing pencil. Then, when you have it drawn correctly, go over everything with a darker drawing pencil. Two things to keep in mind are *plumb lines* and, as mentioned in a previous lesson, *negative space.* Plumb lines are straight lines that show where one part is in proportion to another. These straight lines can be either horizontal, vertical, or diagonal. To use plumb lines in your drawings, take your pencil and, with one eye closed, see the angle of the line from one point to another and draw it correctly on your paper. For example, if you question exactly how high the head of the man on the horse is in proportion to the horse, take your pencil and, closing one eye, see the angle of the line your pencil makes from the top of the horse's head to the top of the man's head, and draw that line on your paper at the exact angle (A). You can also use a plumb line to show the position of the tip of the horse's nose with the top of the rear leg and bottom of the belly (B). Also, do not forget to observe the negative space in certain areas. Again, a good example of this is the area between the horse's head and the neck, or the area between the two forelegs (C).

A.   B.   C.

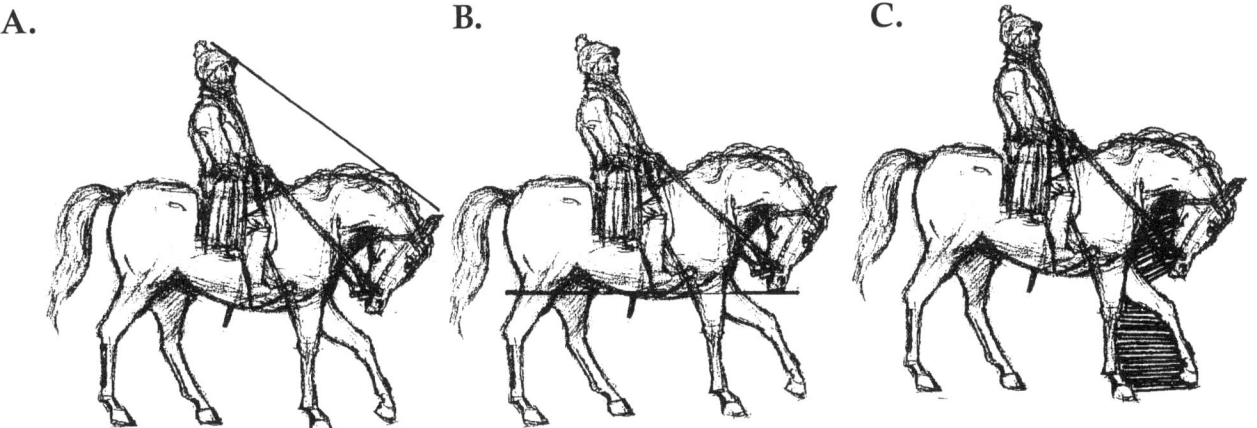

Lesson #51:
Drawing a Statue

For this assignment, draw from a statue of a horse in your sketchbook. This may be difficult to do since you may not have a statue of a horse in your neighborhood. If this is the case, you may want to draw from a toy model of a horse. When drawing from objects which are in front of you, it is a good practice to look up every three seconds to remember what you are drawing. For example: draw, one-two-three, look up, draw, etc. Have a light source and use your *3B* pencil.

Drawing Horses from Life

Certainly, it is ideal to do drawings of your own horse. Yet, most of you probably do not have a horse. If this is the case, see if you can plan outings on Saturdays to a neighbor's farm or ranch, public stables, or even horses that pull carriages and wagons in downtown areas. Try drawing horses from life whenever possible as it can be a great teacher.

As mentioned, it is good to draw horses at more opportune times when they are not moving much. A good time to draw them is while they are resting or laying in the fields. Another good time is while they are eating because they will hold relatively still. Grazing is also a good time as they move slowly, giving you ample time to do your studies. Finally, in the beginning, the best time to draw animals from life is while they are sleeping.

The Best Time to Draw Horses:

1. When they are resting.
2. While they are eating.
3. During grazing.
4. When they are asleep.

A.

B.

At first, instead of concerning yourself with drawing the entire horse (which most often is all but impossible because of their movements), try concentrating on basic features. For example, you may want to draw just the legs, or do a head study, or concentrate on the tail, the eye, the ears, the nose, etc. Notice the study I did of *"Star's"* leg. I had finished everything down to his fetlock and then he moved (A). Well, I simply started drawing another part of his body and left it unfinished. However, the following day, *"Star"* returned to his original position and I was able to finish his leg (B). This is a very good pointer: *If the horse moves while you are drawing him, start doing a study of another feature, or position of the horse, and return to your drawing when the horse returns to its original position.*

Quick Life Studies of Horses

"Quick Studies" by Barry Stebbing

Lesson #52: *A Portrait of a Horse*

Let's go outside and draw the front view of a horse's head from life. When you draw a familiar person's head it is called a *"portrait."* Try to remember the basic shapes when you are drawing. Hopefully, you will have a horse who will pose for you. I found *"Star"* to be an excellent model as he stared at me intently while I drew him. Remember, do not become frustrated if the horse moves. Sit patiently and, quite possibly, he will return to his original position. In the meantime, you can do sketches of other parts of his body. Notice the sketch I did below in Lone Pine, California. I probably spent no more than a minute on each horse.

If you do not have a horse, you can either copy from a picture, or draw a portrait of one of your pets in the figure box above. Use your drawing pencils for this assignment. Practice by doing some small sketches in the figure boxes below and other quick studies in your sketchbook.

"Lone Pine, California" by Barry Stebbing

Lesson #53: *A Grazing Horse*

Remember, one of the best times to draw a horse is while he is grazing or moving slowly. However, a problem students have when drawing a grazing horse is that they either draw the neck too short or the legs too long. Notice the two sketches below (A & B) that I did in a journal entry on page 81. The first one shows that the neck is too short because the horse's head does not touch the ground (A). When drawing a grazing horse, it is important to have the tip of the horse's nose even with the bottom of his hooves (B). You may want to draw a straight line for the ground to make sure that the head and hooves are on the same plain. Also, a rectangular frame is a good start for drawing a horse while grazing (B). Observe the drawing by Sarah Clayton on the bottom of the page, and how she drew a grazing horse correctly (C). For the first part of this assignment, draw a horse grazing in the figure box below. You may copy from one of these illustrations (B or C), or from another picture. Then, take your sketchbook outside and draw at least four studies of horses grazing. Even though horses walk slowly while grazing, they do return to the same pose again and again, making it possible for you to continue with your sketches.

A. This is Wrong

B. This is Correct

C.

"Horse Grazing" by Sarah Clayton Age 16

Lesson #54: *Drawing a Horse Lying Down*

Have you ever noticed horses lying down? This is one way in which they like to rest. A horse in this position is like a boat in water, as you only see part of it. This position should be easy to draw because you can concentrate on the body without drawing the legs. Notice the wonderful drawing of a horse lying down by Julia (below), and that she even included the legs. However, you may find it easier in the beginning to draw just the top part of the horse and not concern yourself with the legs. For this assignment, draw a horse lying down in the figure box below. Draw him just as though he were standing (A) but, shall we say, putting the bottom half of his body "under water," or lying in grass (B). Bring the shoulder out, or rounded a little more, because his legs are hunched closer to his body. Use your colored pencils for this exercise and place tall grass and flowers underneath him.

"Horse Lying Down"
by Julia Smith Age 14

Horse Sense: Start Your Drawings Off Lightly

Lesson #55: *Drawing A Horse Lying Down Part II*

Now let's draw a horse lying down without the tall grass to cover his legs as you did in the previous lesson. Look at the fine drawing of a horse lying down with the legs showing by Tessha (below). Once you know how to draw a horse, it is a simple matter to add the legs in this position.

First, complete the drawing of Tessha's horse by adding the legs (A). Do this by lightly drawing lines for the angles of the legs (B) just as you did in Lesson #27. Then add the flesh around these lines (C). When you are finished, draw the entire horse in the picture frame below with a light colored pencil. Let's suppose the sun is shining from the upper right of the sky (D). Can you show a light side and a shaded side to your horse? Finally, color in your picture with colored pencils and add grass and flowers in the foreground.

"Horse Lying Down"
by Tessha Zimmerman Age 14

Lesson #56: *Adding Values to a Horse*

Values are the different gradations from light to dark that can be used for shading. Many students simply shade areas with one solid dark value. Notice the delightful drawing by Heidi (below). I love her horse, although some areas could be less bold (like the eyes and nostrils), and others could be darker (under the neck).

As mentioned, one way of shading is with lines. And there is more to shading than just having a light side and a shaded side. Your drawings should have many values from *light* to *dark*. Your lightest value is the white of the paper and, from there, you can make darker values by placing lines closer and closer together (A). Your darkest values can be done by *cross-hatching* (B). First, do a *value study* from light to dark (as shown below) using your black pencil and placing values from lightest to darkest in the bottom row of horses. Make sure you have a sharp point, and remember, the closer you put your lines, the darker the value will be. When you are finished, shade in parts of the horse's head below (including the eyes and nostrils), using at least five different values from light to dark, and shade with lines (C).

A. Value Study - Light to Dark   B. Cross-Hatching

C.

"Horse Study" by Heidi Ethertow Age 15

Lesson #57: *Light Side & Shaded Side*

Let's now practice *shading* a horse as we did in Lesson #4. Again, shading helps show *form* as the light areas come forward and the shaded areas recede. Likewise, shading can make certain parts of the body look *round*. After all, a horse is basically round: his head is round, his belly is round, and his legs are round.

When drawing from life, the best time to work outdoors is either in the early morning or late afternoon. This is because the sun has a lower trajectory at this time, casting its light at a better angle for shaded areas (A & B). Around noontime the sun is directly above and does not offer much for the artist as far as interesting shadows are concerned (C). Remember, the shaded side is on the opposite side of the light side. Also, it is good to have a darker outline on the shaded side and a lighter line on the light side. Many students, outline everything with one thick line.

A. Morning Light   B. Evening Light   C. Afternoon Light

There are several ways to shade. As mentioned, one is by *"smudge shading,"* or *"finger rubbing"* (blending in the shaded areas with the side of your pencil or with your finger). Another is by shading with *lines*. The latter is a practice that many of the masters used. Remember, there are basically four types of lines you can use for shading: *horizontal, vertical, diagonal,* and *cross-hatching*. However, the most common and most effective for shading is *diagonal*, because it adds a certain action to your drawing. For this assignment, shade each of the horses below with pencil first, and then with your black drawing pen. Shade the top two horses in the areas outlined (as illustrated above), using horizontal lines for one and vertical lines for the other. Draw a little sunshine with an arrow to show the direction your light is coming from. Then, shade parts of the bottom two horses, shading one with diagonal lines and the other with cross-hatching. Finally, shade the legs in the background of all four horses.

D. Horizontal Lines   Vertical Lines

Diagonal Lines   Cross-Hatching

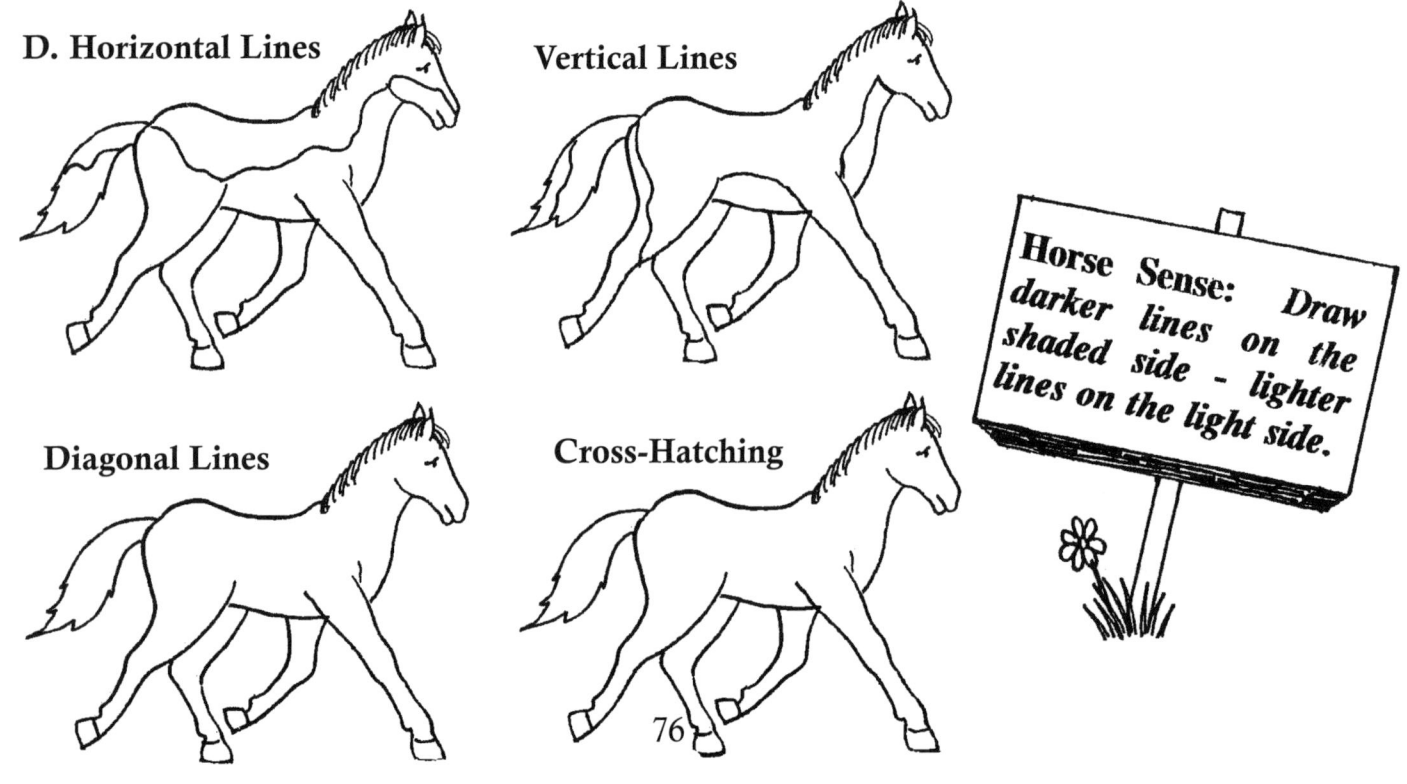

Horse Sense: Draw darker lines on the shaded side - lighter lines on the light side.

Lesson #58: *Stippling*

Stippling sounds like horse terminology, doesn't it? It is actually a drawing term that means drawing with dots. In previous lessons, we learned about shading with lines and values from light to dark. However, there are other ways to shade. One such method is shading with dots. This is a wonderful technique and most students have a great deal of success shading in this manner. For example, take a look at Bethany's horse below and the wonderful job she did shading, using this method. However, just as in Heidi's drawing in Lesson #56, the eyes and nostrils are too dark. Likewise, when stippling, do not outline too much (A), but rather allow the dots to outline parts of the shape (B). Finally, when shading with dots, the closer you place the dots, the darker the value, the farther apart you place the dots, the lighter the value. Observe the delightful horse drawn by Courtney Good (bottom right). She did an excellent job, but she could have made some areas darker by placing her dots closer together.

A. *No!*
B. *Yes!*

For the first part of this exercise, use your black pen to do a value study from light to dark with dots in the row of horses above. Then, shade in some more areas of Bethany's horse below (C), including the eye, with various values. Finally, see if you can add more dots to Courtney's horse (D) to give it darker values.

C.
D.

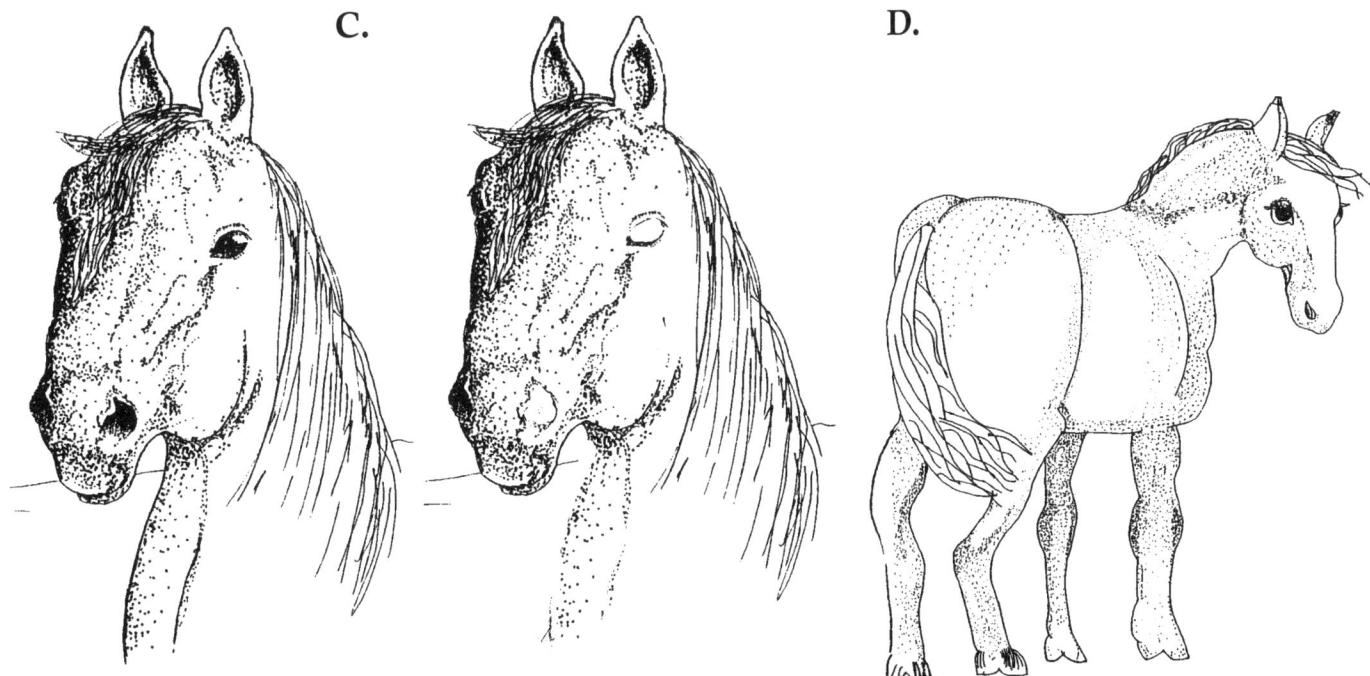

"A Horse" by Bethany Rogers Age 14

"A Horse" by Courtney Good Age 15

Lesson #59: *Coloring a Horse with Light*

Drawing horses in early morning or late afternoon light provides a brilliance of golden color cast upon the horse's hide. Notice the adorable drawing of a horse by Bryson to the left. If you look closely, you will see that he has drawn a light source and even has a highlight on the horse's rump! A very good observation for a 6 year old.

"Horse in Light" by Bryson Ware Age 6

For this assignment, go outside and notice the vivid color on a horse just before the sun sets (during this time there is usually an orange-like color in the light areas of a horse). First, take your orange colored pencil and draw a horse from life in the figure box below. After you have drawn him, lightly outline the areas that are going to be shaded (A). Block the shaded areas in quickly because the sun moves rapidly during this time of the day (B). For now, do not be concerned with how perfect or realistic your horse looks. In this exercise we are more concerned with learning the light and shaded areas, and also seeing the colors on a horse's hide in the light.

A.

As mentioned, you will probably see an orange-like tone on the light areas of the horse's hide. You may want to add a little yellow to brighten the orange. Then lightly go over this bright yellow/orange with brown (or whatever other color the horse may be). For the shaded areas, use more blue and violet (and even a touch of red) instead of black. This will add richness and color to the shaded areas. If you do not have a live horse to draw, copy the horse to the left, and add shading and color. When you are finished coloring in your horse, take the color which the horse is (for example, brown), and *lightly* blend all the colors together with this color. Finally, take your black colored pencil and go over some of the details, such as the eyes, nose, mane, and hooves.

B.

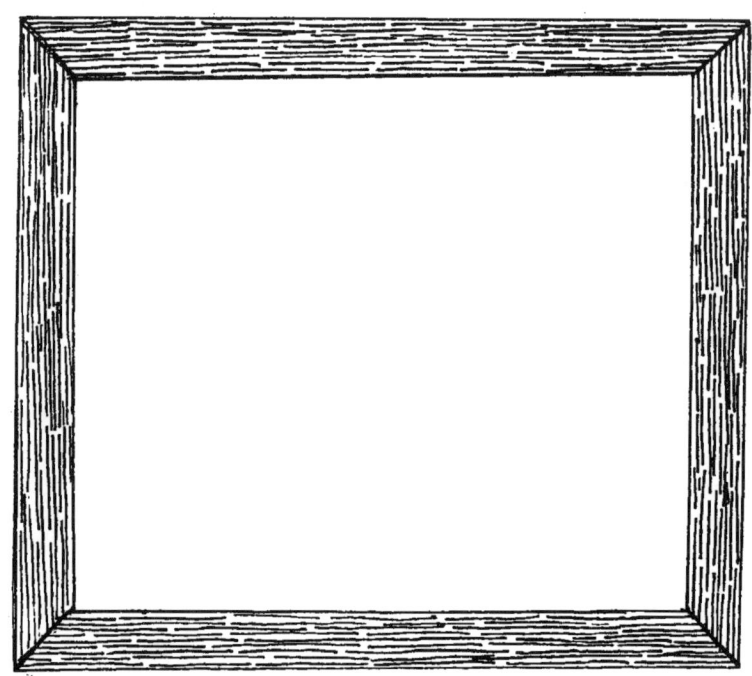

Lesson #60: *Gesture Drawings*

Let's take our sketchbook and go outside to draw more horses from life. Remember, it is not easy to draw live animals in the beginning, so do not become frustrated. You are trying to learn from the experience. I recommend, when working outdoors, that you dress properly, take a portable chair, wear a hat or sit in the shade, and clip your papers down so they won't blow in the wind.

Before going outside, let's do a warm-up exercise with gesture drawings by copying the quick sketches below and on the next page in your sketchbook. Use your *5B* pencil and remember to work quickly, trying to draw the entire horse in about thirty seconds. Stay away from details, simply suggesting the basic form and movement of each horse. Again, take a look at my quick studies below and on the next page, and notice how I worked quickly, simply suggesting many of the smaller features and details of the horses.

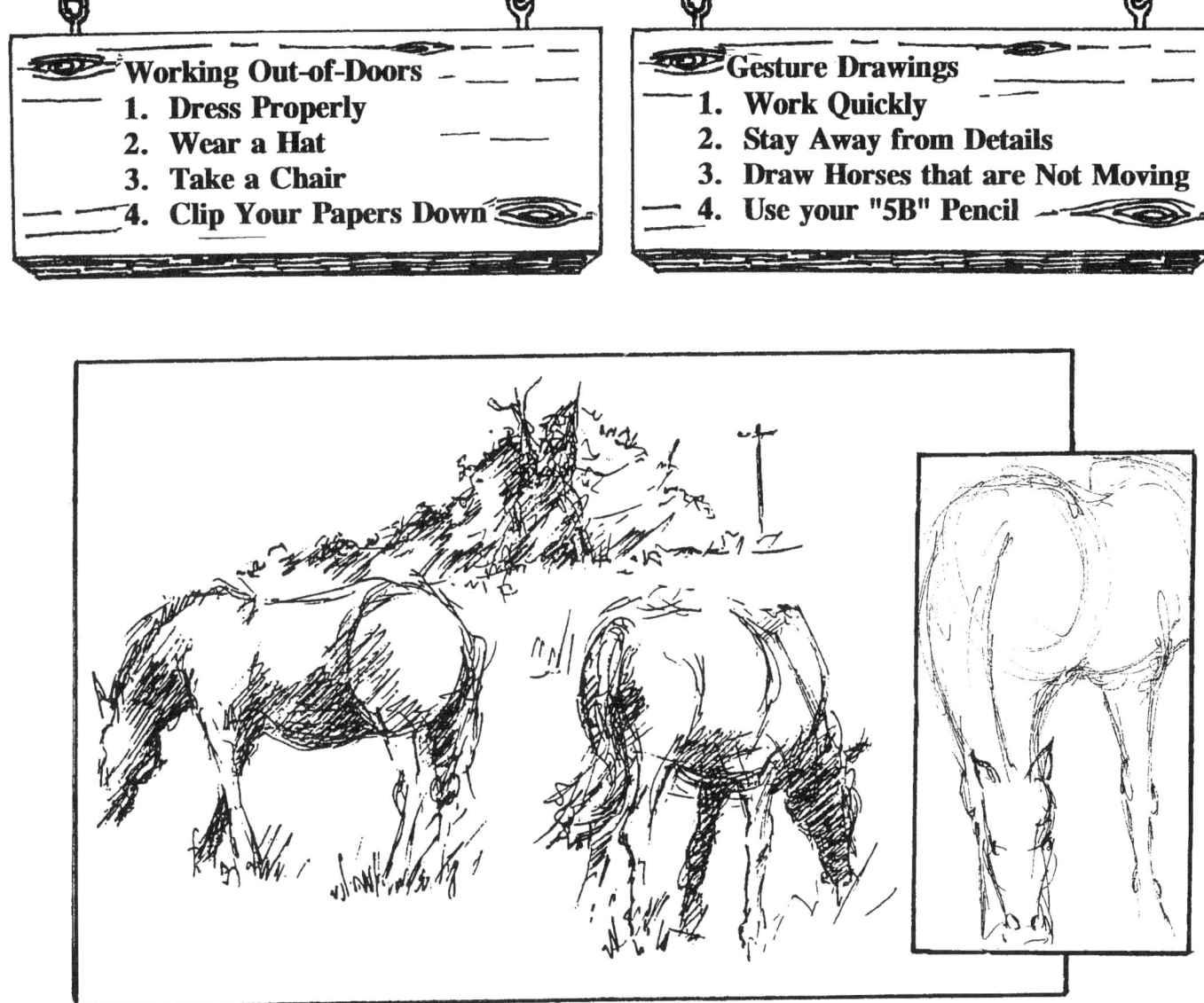

"Quick Studies of Horses" by Barry Stebbing

Lesson #61: *More Gesture Drawings*

Now, go outside and do some more quick *gesture drawings* of either horses or any other pets which you may have, such as cats, dogs, or even a bird or fish. The principle with any pet is the same: you will be drawing a living animal which moves, so work quickly, and stay away from details. Use your *5B* pencil to do these drawings in the figure boxes below. Again, do not become frustrated with this assignment, as you literally have to do hundreds of such drawings before making progress. *Practice! Practice! Practice!*

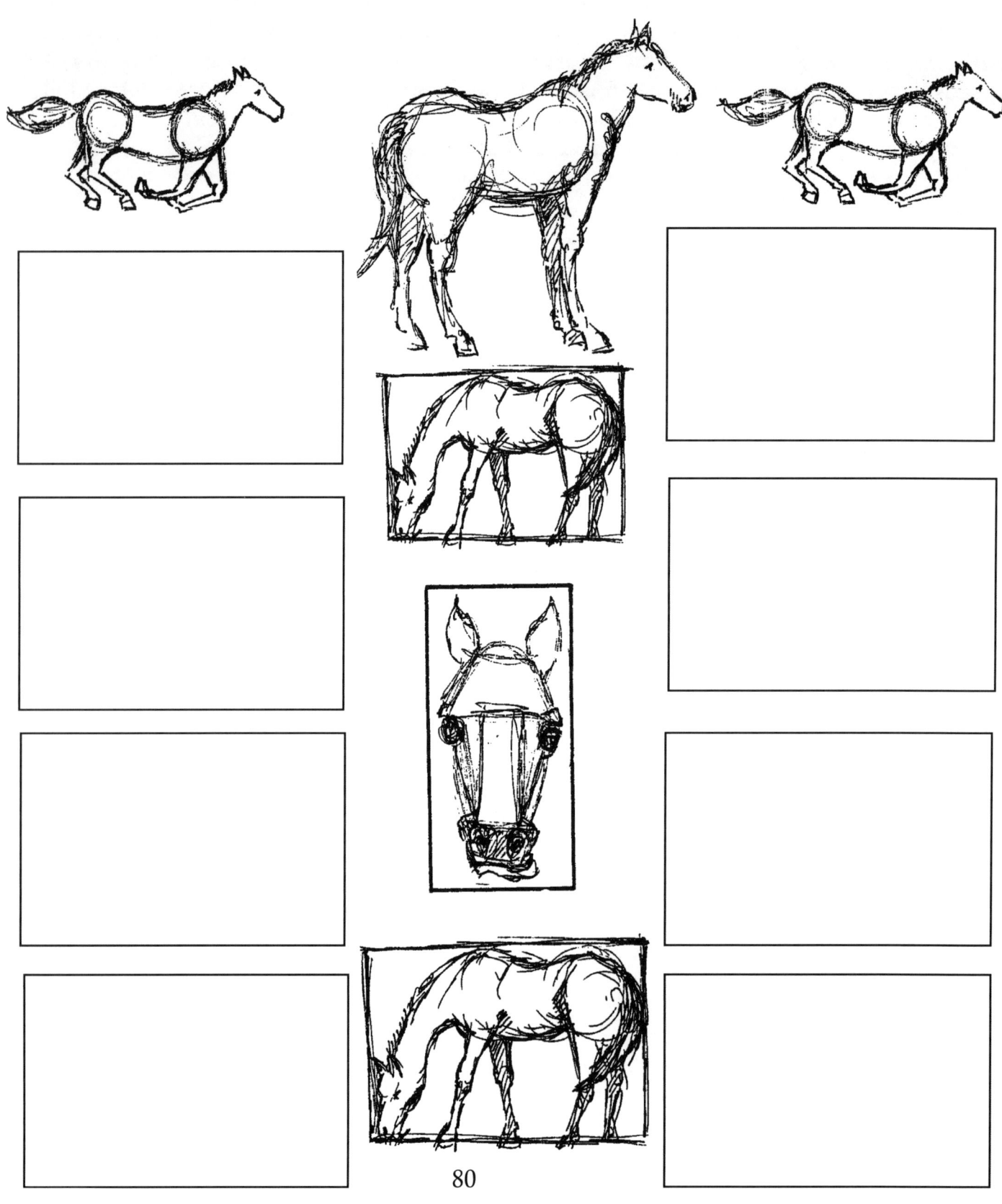

A Page from My Journal…

Keeping an art journal can be a wonderful course of study as it encourages students in many ways. You could even have a "horse" journal as your theme! Below are some suggestions for journaling and a page from one of my journals. Notice that the sketches were done quickly with very little detail. Also, notice that I wrote comments on the page as to what I liked and disliked about the drawings. Remember, drawing from life is an excellent study and can be a great teacher.

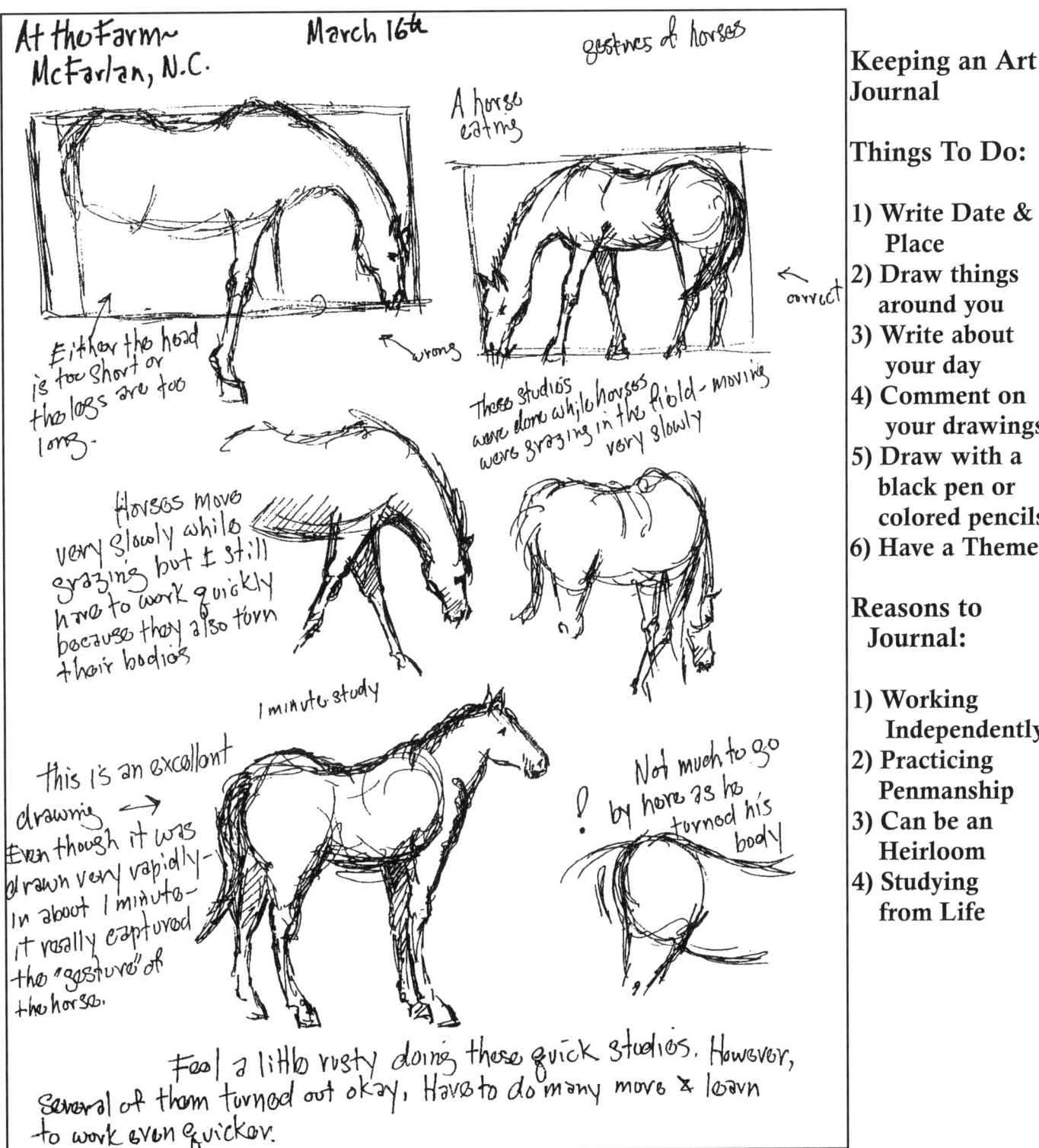

A Day in the Life of...

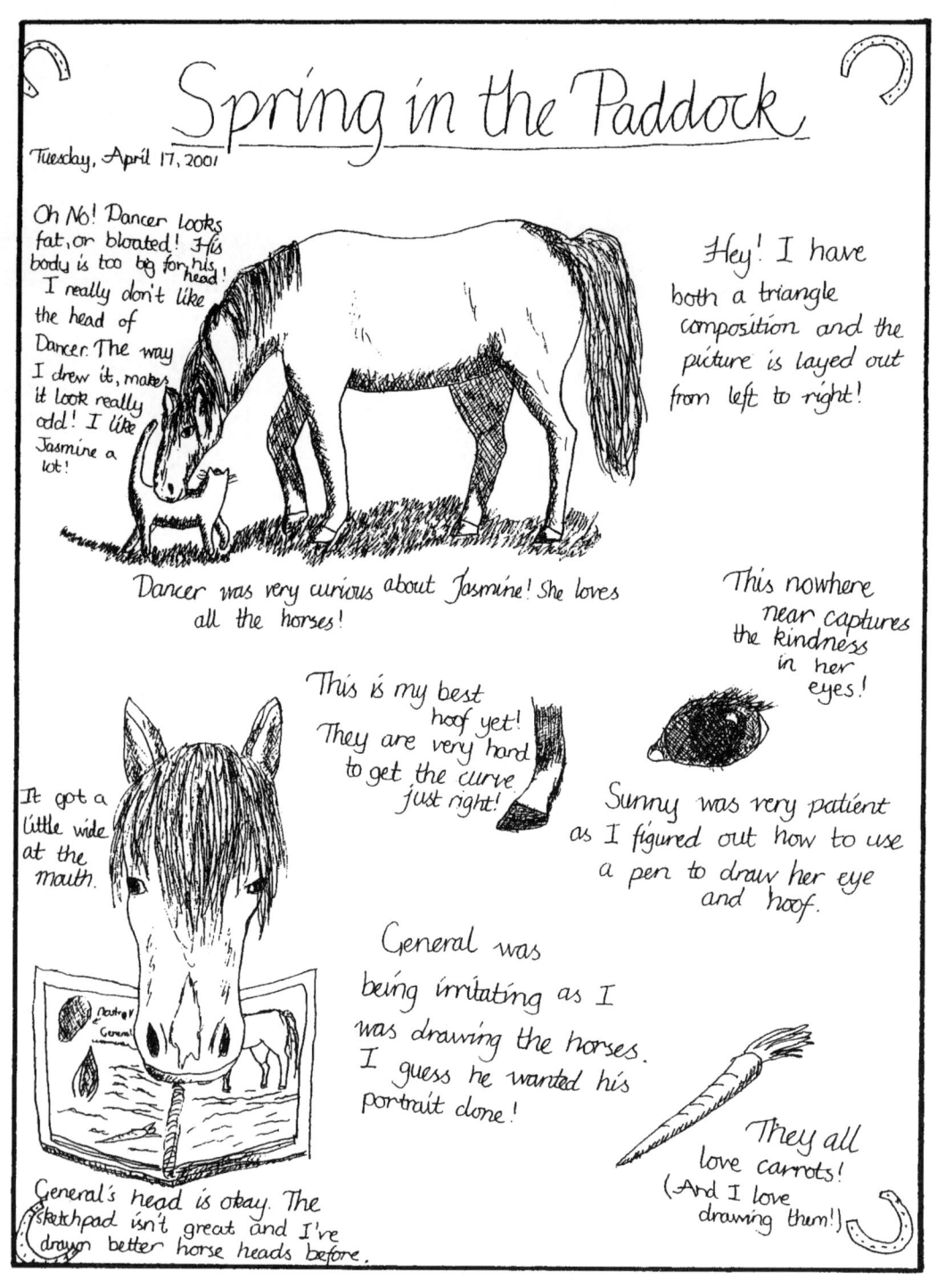

"My Art Journal" by Catherine Rivard Age 11

Observe the delightful drawings from the art journal of Catherine. These were all studies that she did of her horses, "*Sunny*," "*General*," and "*Dancer*." This is certainly a great journal entry.

Journaling is good for students to do because it teaches you to work independently and to observe subject matter from life. It also nurtures good penmanship and generates creativity as the pages fill.

Remember, as a student, you can be your best teacher through observing things around you. Catherine comments in her journal entry of April 17th, that when she drew *General's* head, *"It got a little wide."* Through observation and drawing, she learned to evaluate her own work.

She also commented that the eye she drew did not capture, *"the kindness in her (the horse's) eyes,"* She continued, *"Sunny was very patient as I figured out how to use a pen to draw her eye and hoof."* Notice that she said, *"I figured out!"* And that is how the student learns, from close observation.

Another Day in Catherine's Journal...

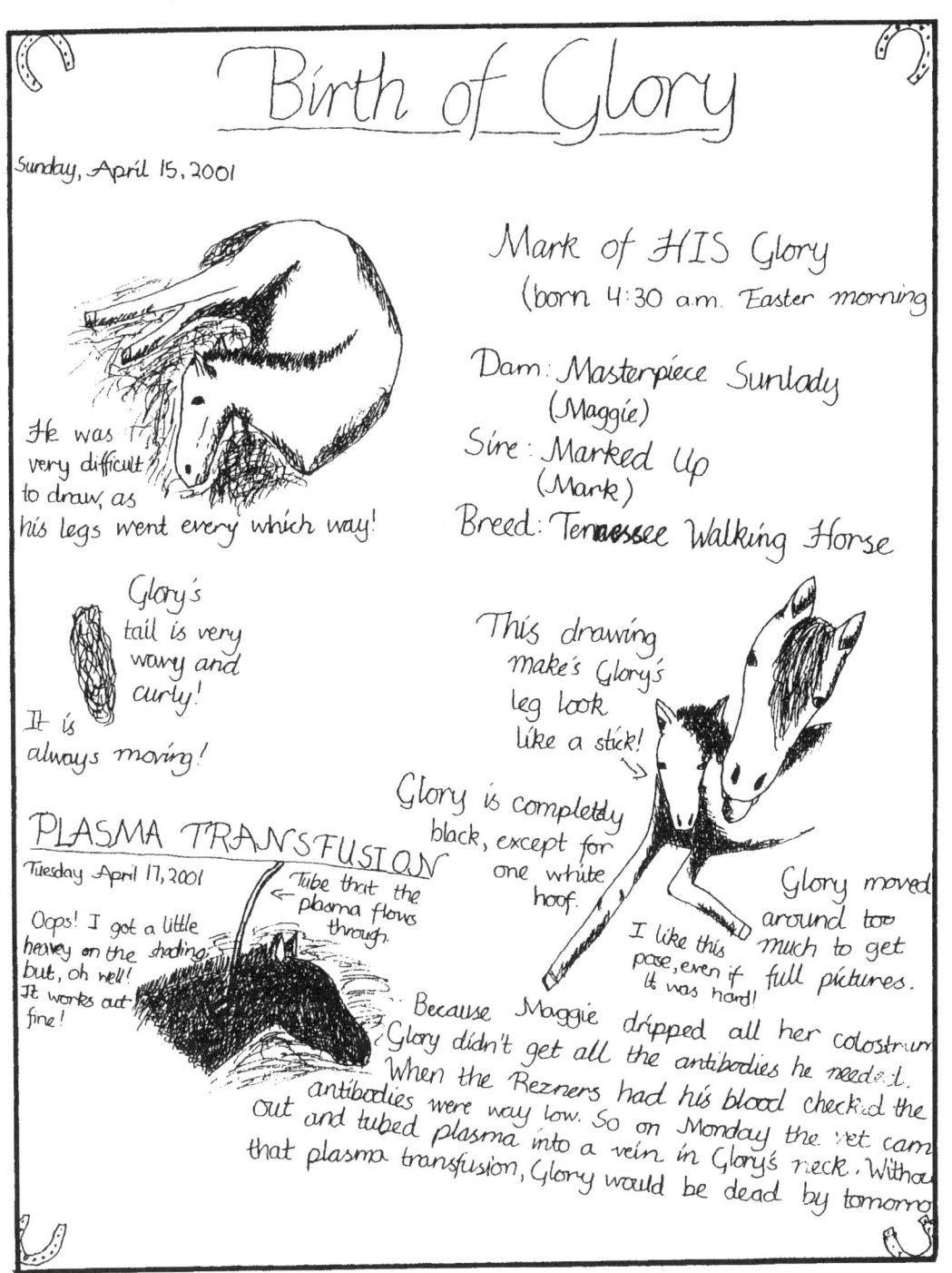

In this entry of Catherine's journal, dated April 15th, she illustrated and wrote about the birth of their new horse, *"Glory."* Catherine admits that the young colt was not easy to draw. *"This drawing makes Glory's leg look like a stick!"* She continued, *"Glory moved around too much to get full pictures."* In other words, she couldn't complete the drawings of *Glory's* body because of all the movement. Even though Catherine's drawing studies of the horses were difficult, she went on to comment, *"I like this pose, even if it was hard."* She went on to comment in this day's entry, *"Glory's tail is very wavy and curly!"*

Catherine also wrote about drawing the newly born colt as he was lying down. *"He was very difficult to draw, as his legs went every which way!"* (You probably found this out when you drew a horse laying down in a previous lesson.)

The most important thing to realize is that even though Catherine had difficulty with some of these life studies, she was *learning*. And that is what we want to do! Remember, drawing is learning through practice. No one creates masterpieces in the beginning, and the more we practice, the better our drawings will be.

Lesson #62: *Keeping an Art Journal*

For this assignment, let's start a horse journal. If you have a horse, write about him and also draw him, the barn, and other things that relate to him. If you do not have a horse, let your journal page be about a pet that you have. Along with drawing and writing about your pet, you can also talk about your day: the weather, how you feel, what you learned, how you like your drawings, etc. Fill the page with drawings and then write about your day on the lines below. Use either pen or colored pencils for your drawings.

Lesson #63: *The Different Positions of a Horse*

For this assignment, see if you can draw a horse in four different positions: front view, rear view, side view, and lying down. You can do this from your imagination, go outside and study from live horses, or copy from drawings in this text or other pictures. Do these with your drawing pencils, starting with your *HB* pencil.

Lesson #64: *Horses in Review*

Most students forget much of what they have learned and go back to their old ways of drawing. That is why reviewing what you have learned is so important. First, let's review the head. (Notice the delightful horse's head by Kirstine below.) Remember, the side view of the head is drawn with a circle for the forehead and a large oval for the nose (A). The ears are leaf-shaped, the eye like a bird flying sideways with a circle in it (B); the forelock and mane are drawn with pointed, curved shapes (C); and the nose is on a slant with tear-drop shapes for the nostrils (D). Draw the horse's head in the figure box (below), reviewing these basic pointers.

A.   B.   C.   D.

Next, let's practice drawing the entire body. The belly is a large oval shape (E), and the shoulders and rump are large circles on either side of the oval (F). The thighs are trapezoids; the *cannon* (lower part of the leg) a thin rectangle; and the hooves are parallelograms (G). For this exercise, see if you can remember all the various parts and, once again, put the parts together to make a horse. Do your drawing in your sketchbook from memory, and see if you can draw the parts without looking at a horse. Start with your orange colored pencil and go over everything with your brown and black colored pencils. Make sure to smooth out some of the lines.

E.

F.

G.

"Horse Study"
by Kirstine Petersen
Age 10

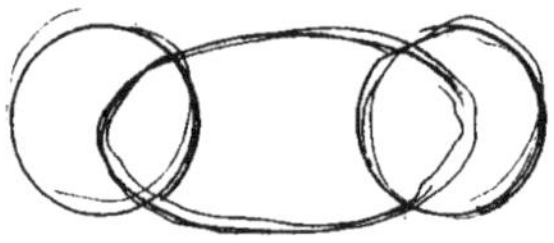

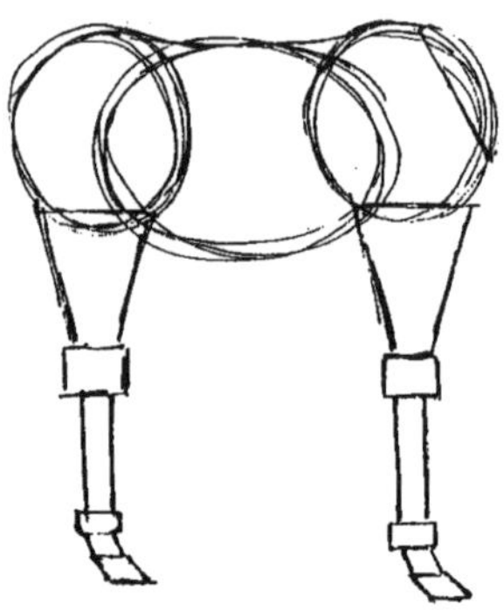

Lesson 65#: *Horse Oats - "The Breakfast of Champions"*

Let's design the cover of a cereal box for horses (after all, horses eat *"cereals"*). Draw a horse's face on the front of your box. You can make it comical (as Kirby's delightful illustration below), or more realistic. Can you give your cereal a catchy name? You may want to start by doing some *thumbnail sketches* in the small cereal boxes to better formulate your design. Draw your final design in the large cereal box below and color it in with your colored pencils. Before beginning, see if you can draw a cereal box on the bottom of the page like those illustrated. Use a ruler and guidelines for all your lettering to make it as professional as possible.

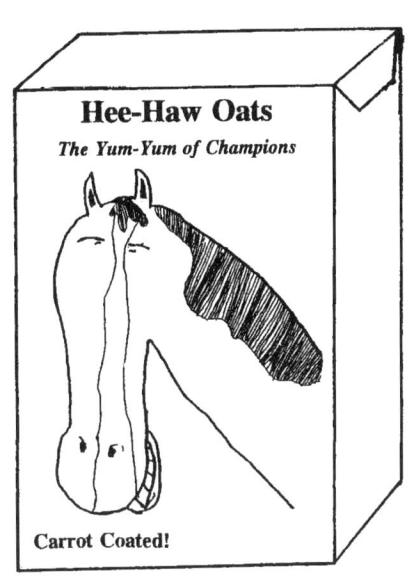

"A Horse" by Kirby Sampson Age 11

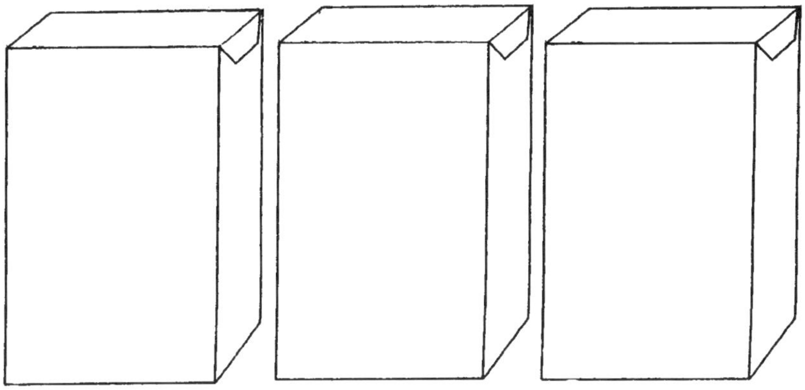

A. Thumbnail Sketches

Draw A Cereal Box Here

Lesson #66: *Examination II*
(Answers may be found by reviewing Part II of text)

I. True or False

_____ 1. The dorsal stripe is a marking on the face of a horse.
_____ 2. The forelock is the front part of the mane that goes over the forehead.
_____ 3. The radius is another name for the ankle of a horse.
_____ 4. The most difficult way to draw a horse is from "life."
_____ 5. When drawing from life the student should look up every three seconds.
_____ 6. Horizontal lines are lines that go up and down.
_____ 7. Values are different gradations in drawing from light to dark.
_____ 8. Cross-hatching is a disease horses obtain from not eating enough oats.
_____ 9. An HB pencil is your darkest drawing pencil.
_____ 10. A trapezoid is a good shape to use for drawing the thigh and neck of a horse.

II. Matching

1. dorsal stripe   a. side view
2. overlapping   b. a dark marking that goes down the rump
3. cannon   c. the space in between parts of an object
4. stippling   d. small, preliminary drawings
5. negative space   e. the long, thin rectangular bottom part of the leg
6. thumbnail sketches   f. placing one object slightly in front of another
7. profile   g. a technique in drawing with dots
8. radius   h. a large leg bone

III. Fill in the Blank

1. _____ _____ are small sketches used to better formulate an idea for a finished drawing.
2. _____ objects can be anything from statues, to monuments, to cast models.
3. Four good reasons to journal are: _____, _____, _____, and _____.
4. The _____ is the part of the hair that goes between the ears and over the forehead.
5. The three ways to draw a horse are: _____, _____, and _____.
6. The four different types of lines you can use for shading are _____, _____, _____, and _____.
7. Name ten parts of a horse:

    1.   6.
    2.   7.
    3.   8.
    4.   9.
    5.   10.

The Wonderful Art of Drawing Horses

Part III
Horse Artists

"Rearing Horse" by Leonardo da Vinci

Horse Artists

You are probably familiar with some great horses that have lived throughout history, such as Robert E. Lee's famous horse, *"Traveller."* And then there was the Lone Ranger's horse, *"Silver."* Almost everyone is familiar with the classic story of *"Black Beauty."* Along with other famous horses which have lived throughout history, there have also been many great horse artists. Studying such artists will help to inspire and educate you in the drawing of horses. Some of these artists, like George Stubbs, concentrated mainly on painting horses. However, there were many other artists who, along with doing artwork on a variety of other subjects, were also masterful at creating horses. These included the great French artist, Eugene Delacroix and the famous Renaissance master, Leonardo da Vinci. There were also great Western artists, like Frederick Remington and Charles Russell, both of whom would be an inspiration to any student who is fond of horses. In this last chapter we will study some of these great masters.

Eugene Delacroix (1798-1863)

As mentioned, there were many artists who were not considered *"horse artists"* but were excellent in their understanding and draftsmanship of the horse. For example, Leonardo da Vinci would not be considered an artist whose entire artistic life revolved around the painting or sculpting of horses. However, this does not negate the fact that he was excellent in drawing them. Another was Eugene Delacroix (del-la-qua), a French artist who lived during the mid-1880s. Delacroix traveled to northern Africa and visited the Arab nations where he was greatly inspired by their costumes and their majestic horses. Delacroix also painted and drew many animals during visits to other countries and zoos, but he seemed to be especially fond of horses. During this time, artists did not have cameras or many pictures to copy from, so most of their drawings were done from life studies. The illustration to the left is a drawing by Eugene Delacroix of an Arab on his black stallion, wonderfully copied by Gregory Iocco. You can see from this that Eugene Delacroix had a great understanding of the horse.

Study of an Arabian on Horseback Eugene Delacroix
Copied by Gregory Iocco Age 14

Lesson #67: *Copying the Masters*

For this assignment, go to the library and copy a horse by Eugene Delacroix in the figure box (left). If you can't find a picture by him, copy the picture above. Start your drawing lightly with your *HB* pencil and then go over it with your black drawing pen. If some of the details in the horse's head seem vague, use various dark values and lines to show subtle variations of shading and also the features. You may want to practice your drawing on another sheet of paper first.

"A Horse"
by Beth Laskowski
Age 9
Rochester, Mn.

Lesson #68: *George Stubbs (1724-1806) - A Great Horse Artist*

George Stubbs was born in England in 1724. As an artist, he was able to portray animals, especially horses, in a heart felt and honest way. George Stubbs was also very creative and innovative, and even painted horses on ceramic surfaces. He was the first artist to publish a book about horses titled, *"Anatomy of the Horse."* Like the French artist, Eugene Delacroix, Stubbs was most interested in action and the violence of conflict, such as lions attacking horses. (Notice the excellent student copy of a Stubb's painting below by Amber).

Stubbs was not recognized as a prominent artist during his lifetime, being labeled simply a *"horse artist."* However, in the mid-part of the twentieth century, he began to be praised and recognized as a truly great artist.

For this assignment, use your sketchbook and see if you can draw a horse in action like the one below of a lion attacking a horse. You may want to go to the library and find an action picture by Stubbs to copy. Or you may select any other action picture. However, if you cannot find a good action picture, you may want to copy the drawing below. Start with a light cream or tan colored pencil. Then, when you have your drawing laid in correctly, go over it with your brown and black colored pencils in some of the areas. Brown and black pencils will give your drawing an old, rustic feeling. Never use a drawing pencil with your colored pencils as the lead is shinier and not very agreeable with the soft lead of the colored pencils.

"Horse Attacked by Lion" George Stubbs - copied by Amber Allen Age 17

Charles Russell - a Cowboy at Heart

Charles Russell was born in 1864 in St. Louis, Missouri. As a boy he longed to go West and, as soon as he was 16, he crossed over the Mississippi River and pursued his dream of becoming a cowboy.

One of his first friends was a mountain man named Jake Hoover whom the young Russell met in Montana. The seasoned mountain man took in the boy, often providing him with a place to stay and meals for months at a time. The wise veteran of the West also gave the young boy encouragement and good advice for the new lifestyle he so desired.

"Rough Riding" Sketch by Charles Russell

Several years later Charles Russell took on a job as a wrangler on cattle drives. This would be a profession that he would have for some time, even though he was not a very good cattle wrangler. Russell spent much of his free time sketching the cattle, horses, cowboys, Indians, folklore, and stories of the wild West. Everyone began to love his artwork of the life and times of the West, and he grew in popularity. Charles Russell never had a formal education in art, and yet his drawings and paintings contained a great understanding of anatomy - both of horse and man. They could also be humorous storytelling of how life was during that time for the cowboys, as illustrated in his drawing below, *"Race for the Grub Wagon."* However, he is best known for the action in his artwork. Notice the quick sketch by Russell of a horse bucking its rider (above).

One thing that he experienced was the changing of the old West. This drastic change in the land and lifestyle took place between 1880 and 1890 as the last of the Indian tribes had been defeated and the white man became more civilized. People began wearing store bought clothes, and the Northern Pacific railroad which crossed the Montana territory from east to west, was finally linked on September 9th, 1883. For Charles Russell, cowboy life had passed away by 1893.

In 1896 he married Nancy Cooper, and traded in his buckskins for a more civilized lifestyle. Charles Russell had always been unsure of his abilities as an artist, but his wife believed in him and began promoting his work. Having difficulty selling paintings in Montana at that time, they moved to New York where he was finally discovered and eventually became one of America's leading Western artists. Charles Russell died in 1926, leaving a legacy of great Western art for all to enjoy.

"Race for the Grub Wagon" by Charles Russell

Artwork by Melody Brohinsky Age 16

Lesson #69: *Horses in Action*

You have drawn horses running in Lesson #26, and horses in violent action in Lesson #67. Now, let's see if you can draw a horse rearing as often seen in pictures of the old West, something that Charles Russell was excellent at doing. You may want to draw a horse rearing on it's hind legs as Melody and Michelle have so wonderfully illustrated (left and below). You may want to copy a drawing by Charles Russell or any other picture you like. Or you can draw your horse from your imagination. Do your drawing below with your drawing pencils. Start with your *HB* pencil and, when you have your horse drawn in correctly, go over it with your darker drawing pencils. Can you add a light source and shade the darker areas with lines?

Artwork by Michelle Traxler Age 11

Lesson #70: *Frederick Remington - an artist of the American West*

Frederick Remington was born in Canton, New York, on October 1st, 1861. Like Charles Russell, he is best known for his artwork depicting the American West as it was in the old days with cowboys, Indians and, naturally, horses. As a boy, Remington did not care too much for formal schooling, spending most of his spare time drawing. He did attend Yale University where he excelled more in athletic endeavors than in the academics. When his father died, Frederick came into a small inheritance and immediately headed west. During this first venture, he traveled through Kansas, North and South Dakota, Wyoming and Montana where he held a variety of jobs, including that of a cowboy. Remington continually sketched the wild west at every opportunity. However, he eventually ran out of money. At the same time he married Eva Caten. With no money and newly married, the couple decided to return to New York and sell his artwork of cowboys and Indians. At first, Remington struggled in this new endeavor, but by 1886 his work began to be published in prominent magazines. From then, until his death in 1909, Frederick Remington was one of the most popular artists of the old west.

Remington was not only a master at drawing and painting cowboys and Indians but also an excellent horse artist. For this assignment, go to the library and study Frederick Remington and Charles Russell. Then, copy one of your favorite pieces of artwork by one of the artists in the figure box on the next page. Place the artist's name and the title of the work on the lines above the picture. Finish by writing about the two artists, their lives, which artist you like best, and why.

"Broncos & Timber Wolves" by Frederick Remington

Remington vs. Russell - Two Great Western Artists

On the lines below, write a report comparing the two artists. Which artist do you like best? Why? Whose horse drawings and paintings do you like best? Why? Was there anything else you found interesting about their lives? Use good penmanship when writing your report.

_____
_____
_____
_____
_____
_____
_____
_____
_____
_____
_____
_____
_____
_____
_____
_____
_____

Name:_____ **Title:**_____

Lesson #71: *Drawing a Story*

Can you tell an old Western story in a drawing the way Remington and Russell did? See if you can draw such a picture in your sketchbook. You may want to pick a title like *"Ol' Indian Joe,"* or *"Rattler,"* or anything else you like! Use your drawing pencils or your black drawing pen and make sure to draw a horse in your picture, drawing in a lot of details.

Leonardo da Vinci & A Very Large Horse

Leonardo da Vinci was born in the town of Vinci on April 15th, 1452. In the history of art, he is certainly considered to be one of the truly great masters, his painting of the *Mona Lisa* being one of the premier paintings of all times. But Leonardo had many other interests besides art including architecture, mathematics, hydraulics, geology, technology, etc. The many fields he applied his abilities to are so varied and diverse that he is known as the best example of renaissance versatility - doing many things in a great manner. It is through him that the term *"Renaissance Man"* has become popular. Certainly, a man for all seasons.

Leonardo was very meticulous in whatever he did, giving everything thorough research. He was a student of observation and, through this, became his own best teacher. However, since he was involved in many endeavors at the same time, and also very meticulous in both his investigations and artwork, much of what he started remains incomplete. It is not that Leonardo was not determined to complete everything, but he was also in great demand. Sometimes the nobility of various towns, cities, or even other countries hired him for military or civil inventions, requiring much of his time and energy.

The last three years of Leonardo's life were spent as a guest of the king of France. At this time it is said that he was paralyzed in his right hand. However, Leonardo da Vinci, the great "Renaissance Man" that he was, was also ambidextrous and able to continue his endeavors with his left hand until his death in 1519.

Horse Study
by
Leonardo da Vinci

"Copy and re-copy the masters." Edgar Degas

Lesson #72: *Studying a Great Master*

If you look closely at Leonardo da Vinci's drawings of horses you will see that he made many observations of them. Mind you, back in the 1500s there were no cameras or pictures to copy from. So, most of these were life studies of horses. You may also notice in his drawings that he made several mistakes. This is especially evident in the placement of some of the legs (as illustrated in the drawing below.) Even though he made mistakes he would continue to finish his drawings.

Edgar Degas was a great French artist who lived during the 1800s. One of his best recommendations for art students was to, *"Copy and re-copy the masters."* This is excellent advice as it will teach the student not only the methods of these great artists but also, a little of their thought process. There is a big difference between simply copying from a picture, as we have done in previous lessons, and copying from a drawing done by one of the great masters. On the proceeding pages are many of the drawings that Leonardo da Vinci did of horses. These are an excellent study for you to copy. As you draw from them, you will learn much about his techniques, such as shading with line, the delicacy and beauty of his lines and composition. Even his thought process is evident in some of these works. For this assignment, copy all of da Vinci's drawings of horses on the next several pages in your sketchbook. Use your drawing pencils and start off lightly.

"Horse Study" by Leonardo da Vinci

Leonardo da Vinci was a great observer of life. He shows us that we can learn by observing. Through his studies of life, Leonardo created some of the best art journals in the history of man. Did you know that he completed over seven thousand pages in his art journals? As mentioned, one of the reasons we encourage students to keep an art journal is that it will help you become a student of observation, studying and drawing the things which are around you.

Not only was Leonardo a man of many great abilities but he used these abilities in a wide range of areas. However, his most talented area was in the masterpieces of art which he created. As far as horses are concerned, he was involved in creating the greatest horses of all time. Over five hundred years ago, Leonardo da Vinci was commissioned by a wealthy duke of Milan to create a large bronze horse. This was to be the largest statue of a horse ever constructed. It was to weigh over 80 tons and would stand 24 feet tall. The name of this horse sculpture was, *"Il Cavallo,"* which means, *"The Horse."* The creation of this horse was one of Leonardo da Vinci's greatest dreams. Unfortunately, he was only able to complete the first stage, which was a full-scale model in clay. It was destroyed by French archers when they invaded Milan in September of 1499. Leonardo died leaving his great creation unfinished. Yet, many of his sketches of *"Il Cavallo"* still remain (as illustrated below), but his great dream would lay incomplete until this century.

In 1977, an American art collector, Charles Dent, was inspired to complete the unfinished work of Leonardo. He decided that both Italy and Leonardo deserved the finished dream. So he sponsored sculptors to make the large horse and, after 21 years *"Il Cavallo"* was finally completed (the same amount of time it took to create the Statue of liberty). The large horse was completed 500 years to the day after it's destruction and is displayed in the city of Milan where it was originally planned to be located.

Horse Study
  by
Leonardo da Vinci

Leonardo's Horses

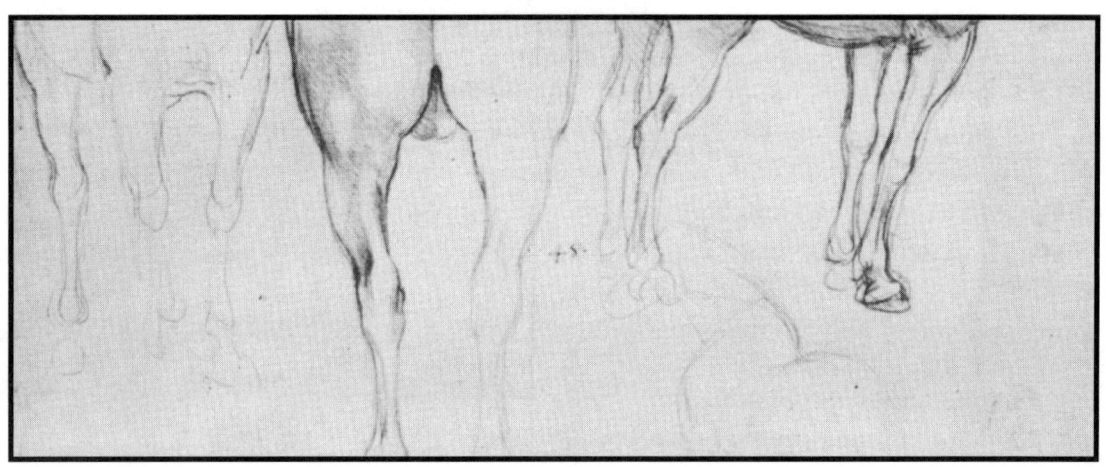

Leonardo's Horses

101

Leonardo's Horses

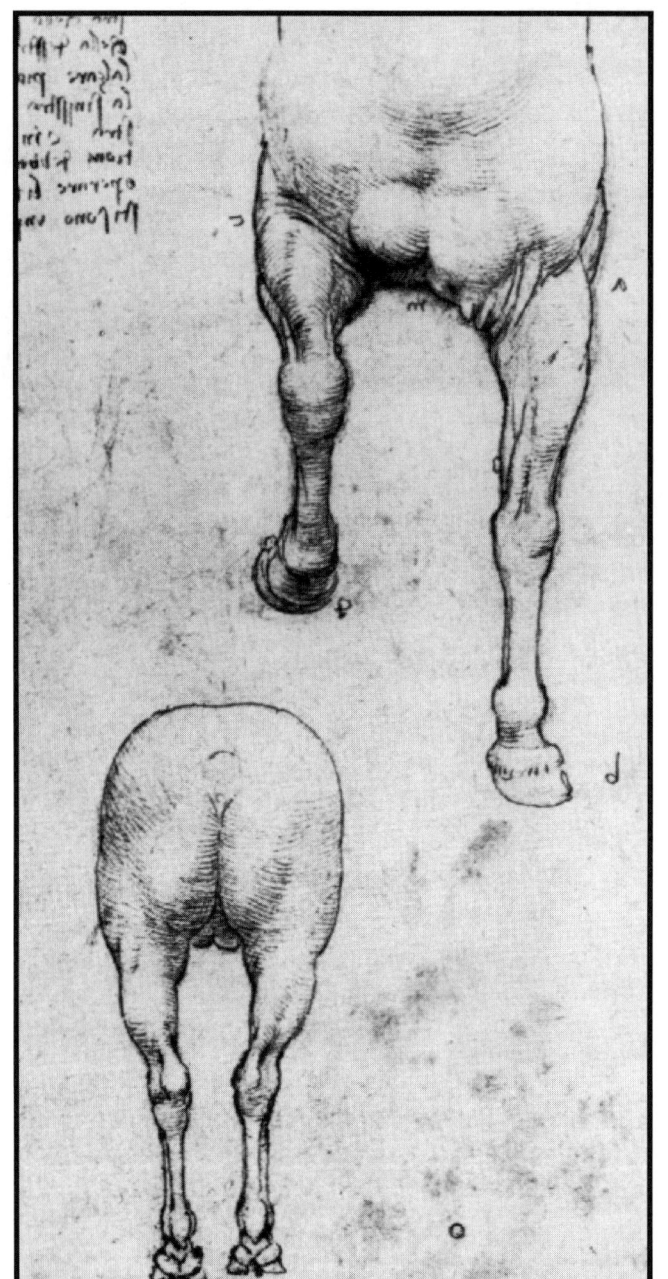
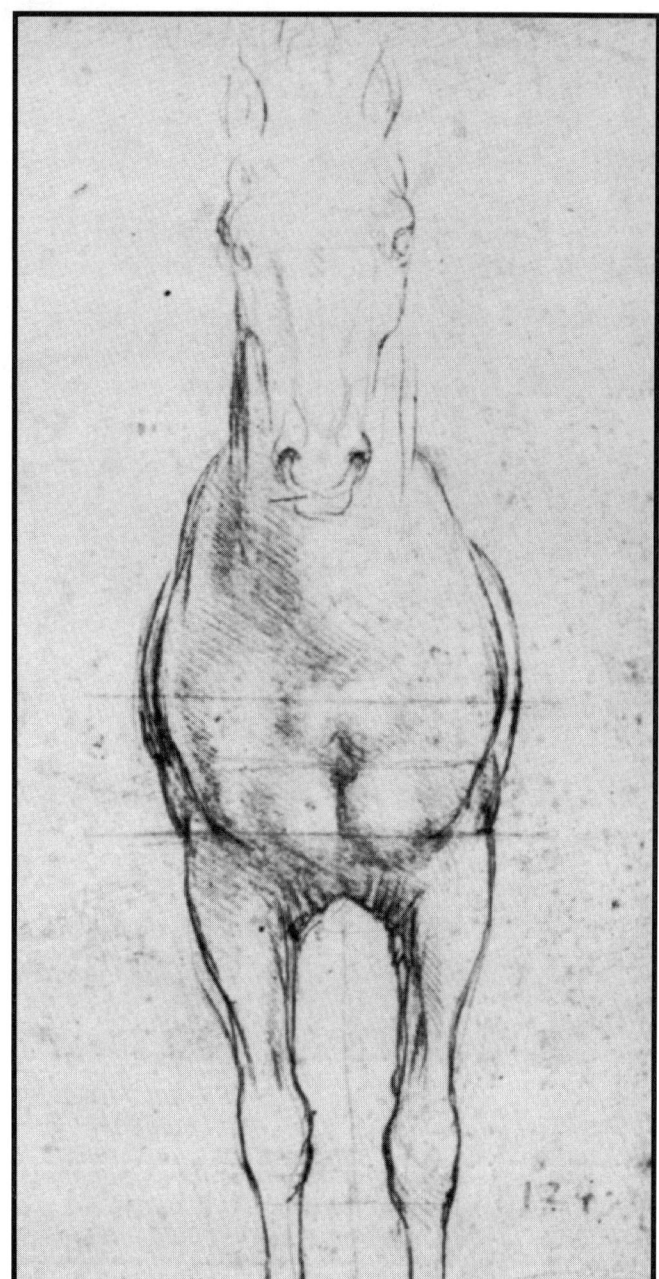
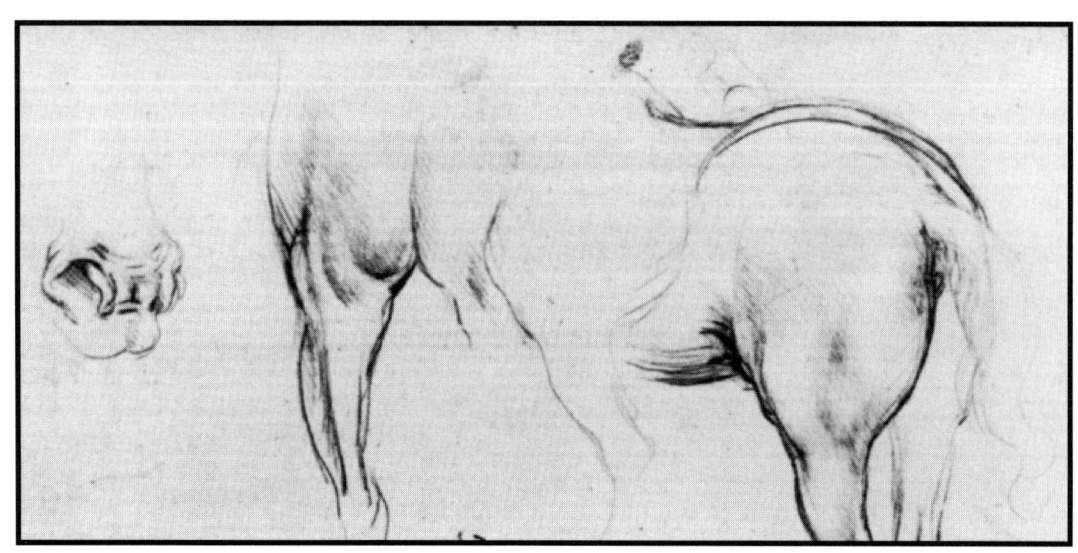

Leonardo's Horses

Lesson #73: *What Do You Think?*

Now that you have copied many of da Vinci's horse drawings, write what you have learned from the experience on the lines below. What did you learn? Do you think he was a great horse artist? What was your favorite drawing by him? Did you notice the beauty of his lines?

Lesson #74:

A Horse is a Horse is a Horse

Now that we are nearing the end of the text, let's draw a horse just as we did in the first lesson. Notice the excellent horse by Justin to the left. Do you know what type of *lines* he used for his darker values? Draw your horse looking in the same direction as you did in the first drawing in Lesson #2. Place a barn in the background and a fence in the foreground. Also, draw some flowers and grass in the foreground. Have a light source and shade parts of your horse. Use your colored pencils for this assignment.

"Horse Study" by Justin Frost Age 13

My Horse Picture   **By:** _____

Independent Studies

Lesson #75: *Circus Horses* For this assignment, draw a circus horse. Put a costume on it and place it in the circus.

Lesson #76: *Horse & Buggy* Can you draw a horse and wagon? See if you can attach a wagon or buggy to the rear of your horse.

Lesson #77: *A Flying Horse* Draw a flying horse! You may want to put it in the clouds and give it wings.

Lesson #78: *A Famous Horse* Do you have a special "famous horse?" You can draw "Black Beauty", or "National Velvet", or any other famous horse that you like.

Lesson #79: *A Swimming Horse* Did you know that horses can swim? For this assignment, draw a horse swimming in the water.

"Circus Horse" by Caitlin Bryan Age 10

Lesson #80: *Horse Cents* Since you love horses, wouldn't it be great if we had horse money! Design some horse coins and dollars with your black pen, placing a horse on all of your new currency.

Lesson #81: *Cut it Out* For this assignment, take colored paper and do large, colorful cut-out pictures of horses.

"Horse & Hitch"
by William B. Finnell II Age 10

"Theophilus" by Lumez Tuggy

Student Art Gallery

Horse Drawing by Christopher Youngdale Age 13

Horse Drawing by Megan Phillips Age 15

Horse Drawing by Cherita Longenecker Age 13 1/2

Horse Drawing by Anna Youngdale Age 11

Horse Drawing by Jodi Swihart

106

Lesson #82:
A Poem about Horses

For the last lesson of this text write a poem about horses! Use the lines on the bottom of the page and see how creative and poetic you can be! Notice the delightful poem below by Jenny Butters. When you are finished, draw some small horse pictures around your poem.

"Three Horses" by Jessica Bremseth Age 11

Horses

Horses are pretty,
Some are even giddy.

I like the Clydesdale,
But some look very pale.

They like to graze,
Even on Saturdays!

They like to eat apples,
Their horseshoes make loud crackles.

by Jenny Butters Age 9

The Wonderful Art of Drawing Horses

Part IV
Coloring Horses with Markers

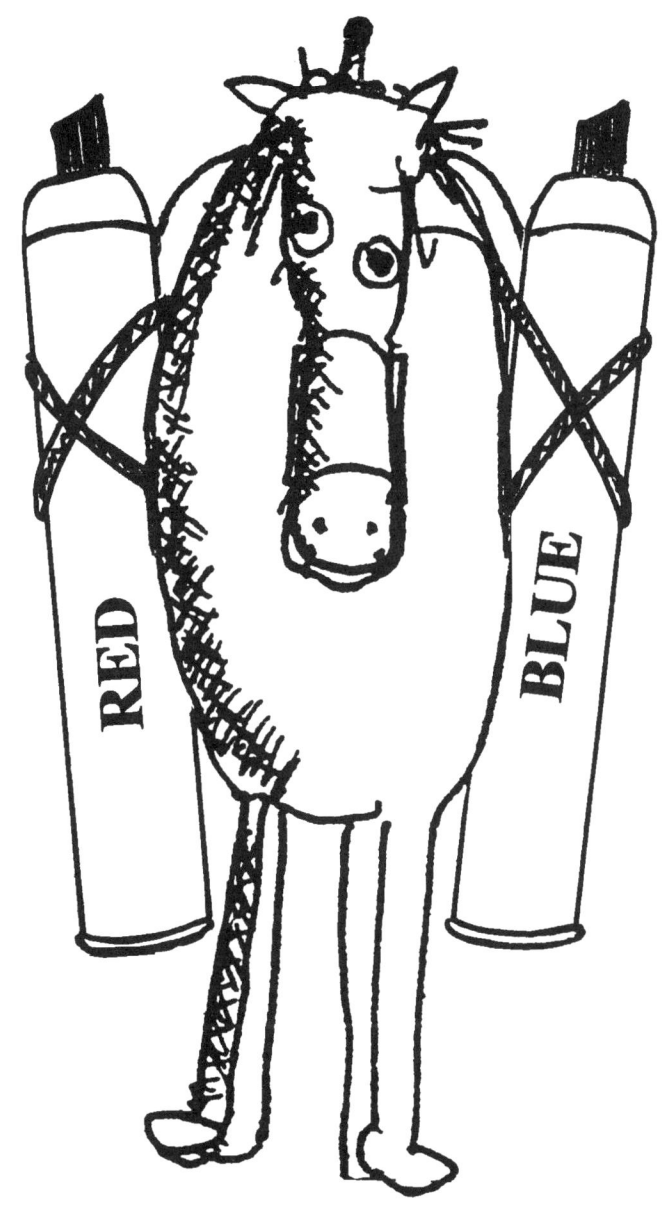

"A Horse" by John Moist Age 6

"The purest and most thoughtful minds are those which love color the most." Ruskin

Coloring with Markers

Now that you have learned all about horses, let's learn how to color them with markers! Coloring with markers can be enjoyable and also give you a whole new type of coloring. Colored markers are a wonderful medium for coloring with *lines* and *dots*. You can even practice beginning painting with them. Colored markers always make bright colors and bold strokes!

Notice that you have five *"marker cards"* which accompany the text. These will be used for the colored marker exercises because they are a thick, cover stock paper which will not bubble up, nor will the colors seep through to the other side. It is recommended that you do not use your colored markers in this text as it is a thinner paper and the colors will seep through to the other side. If, however, you desire to color some of the pictures in *The Wonderful Art of Drawing Horses* with your markers, you should make a copy of the page (preferably on a thicker paper) and use your markers on that. Also, always start with your lightest colored markers (yellow, then orange, then red, and so forth). Drawing with your yellow colored marker will help cut down on mistakes as you can always put darker colors over it. Finally, always remember to put the tops back on your markers as it will prevent them from drying out.

Pointers for Coloring with Markers:

1. Always start with your lightest colors.
2. Remember to put the tops back on the markers.
3. Try to color on a thick stock paper.

Lesson #83: Marker Card #1

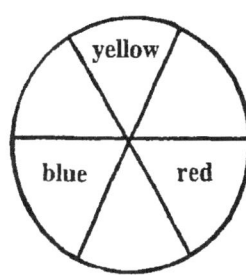
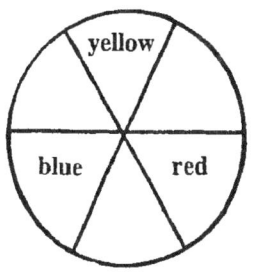

Place *Marker Card #1* in front of you. Also, place a brush and a paper towel to one side and a cup of water above your *marker card*. To begin, color in the two plain circles on the top of your marker card with your colored markers. Color the one in the upper left corner orange and the one in the upper right corner brown.

A.   B.

Next, color in the two color wheels just above the horses (#1 & #2). A *color wheel* teaches us about color theory. Start by coloring the color wheel to the left (#1). First, color in the 3 *primary colors* (yellow, red, and blue) as indicated. In between them color in the *secondary colors* (orange, purple, and green). Orange goes in between yellow and red; purple between red and blue; and green between blue and yellow. Before beginning, color the color wheel above (A) with your colored pencils.

Next, color in the color wheel above the horse to the right (#2) on your *marker card,* but this time color it with *vertical lines* just as you did in Lessons #4 and #58. (As mentioned, vertical lines go straight up and down). Again, start by coloring in the three *primary colors*. Skip a space in between each and color in the three *secondary colors: orange, purple,* and *green*. However, use yellow and red vertical lines to make orange (coloring the pie shape in between the yellow and the red). Do the same in between the red and blue with vertical lines to make purple and then, again, in between the blue and yellow to make green. Before doing this with your markers, practice on the color wheel above (B) with your colored pencils.

Now, let's create a *Pinto* and a *Spotted* horse just as you did in Lesson #5. Take your brown colored pencil and draw and color some large spots on one of the horses below to create a *Pinto*. Then, draw and color some smaller spots on another horse to create a *Spotted horse*. (Add a little orange to the brown spots in your Pinto and some black to the smaller brown spots on the Spotted horse). You have a third horse to color in case you make a mistake.

Next, take your brown pencil and draw large spots on the small horse on the top of your *marker card* (next to the Pinto) and smaller spots on the other horse (next to the Spotted horse). Color in the spots on the Pinto by blending your orange and brown colored markers together and for the Pinto by blending your brown and black colored markers. Remember, always start with your lightest color. Create a Pinto and a Spotted horse by drawing spots on the larger horses with your brown colored marker. Then, take your brush and dip it in water and rub it in the orange circle (you colored on the top of your *marker card*) and paint the first horse a very light orange. Take your brush and dip it in water again and rub it in the brown circle and blend this over the pale orange, giving you a light brownish/orange horse. Finally, take your orange and brown markers and color in the large spots. For the spotted horse, color in the dots by blending your brown and black markers together.

Lesson #84: Marker Card #2

Place *Marker Card #2* in front of you. In Lesson #23 we learned how to put *facial markings* on horses. Let's do this again with our colored markers! First, see how many of the five different markings you can remember by placing them on the horses below (A). Draw the markings lightly with your brown colored pencil. (If you don't remember some of the markings refer back to Lesson #23.) Leave each marking white but color the remainder of the horses' heads by blending several colors together to make various browns. You can even make a blue/black by blending blue with black. When you are finished, select the correct name for each marking (B) and print the marking of each horse on the lines below with your black colored pencil. Underneath that, print the colors you used to color each horse a new color.

A.

B. snip
star
blaze
stripe
freckled

Now, let's complete the horse below (C) with your yellow colored pencil just as you did in Lesson #24. Do you want to put any markings on the horse's head? What about his legs, as we did in Lesson #22? How about a saddle? After you have finished with the details, color him in with your colored pencils. Again, can you make a creative brown by mixing several of your colors together like orange, brown, and yellow? Practice making browns on the two little horses on the bottom of the page.

C.

Start Lightly.

Pinto or Spotted?

Saddle?

Mix Your Colors.

Next, color in the six little horses on the bottom of your *marker card*. Color them with your brown, yellow, orange, black, red, and purple colored markers. Then, color in the five horses' heads on your *marker card*. First, take your yellow colored marker and draw the markings on each. (As mentioned, it is always good to start off lightly with your lightest marker. This will prevent mistakes and allow you to put darker colors over it.) After you have completed the markings take your brush and dip it in water and rub it in the various colors of the small horses on the bottom of the *marker card*, painting each horse a light color. You may want to take your wet brush and rub it in orange and then brown to make a brownish/orange, blue and black to make a bluish/black, and so on. Experiment to see what new, light colors you can make. Make sure not to color the markings. Finally, take your yellow marker and draw the rest of the horse in the middle of your *marker card*. Don't forget to draw markings and other details. Then, take your orange and brown markers and color in the horse, except for the markings. (For his mane and tail you may want to use yellow and orange.)

A.

Finally, take a pencil and ruler and draw a picture frame around your finished horse. Go over it with your black pen when finished and then color it with your orange and brown markers. Draw with broken lines close together to suggest a wooden texture (A). Finally, sign your masterpiece with your brown colored pencil in the bottom center of you picture.

Lesson #85: Marker Card #3

B.

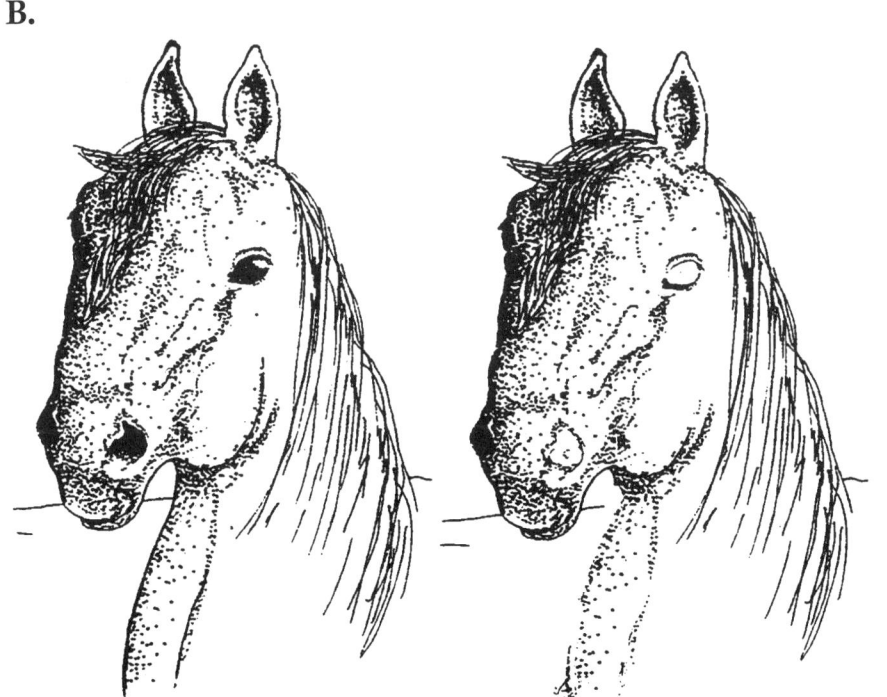

Place *Marker Card #3* in front of you. For this assignment, we are going to color the horses with dots, or *pointillism*. This is similar to Lesson #58. However, you will find that coloring with markers will give you larger dots than with colored pencils or your black pen. Sometimes you will not have as much control because of the thickness of your marker points, but you will make up for this with beautiful colors!

"A Horse" by Bethany Rogers Age 14

First, color the large circles on the bottom of your *marker card* with green, blue, yellow, orange, brown, and black. Next, take a wet brush and rub it in the blue circle and paint a light blue sky behind the two large horses. Wet your brush again and rub it in the green circle and paint a light green for the trees behind the two horses. Next, take a wet brush and rub it in orange and paint the orange stripe of land that is beneath the trees. Wet your brush again and rub it in yellow, orange, and brown and paint the rest of the field with this blend of colors. When you are finished, rub a wet brush in black and neatly paint in two of the smaller horses above this picture with a light, blackish color.

A.

B.

Select two colored markers and color in the smaller horses with dots. Try orange and brown, red and brown, yellow and brown, blue and black, etc. See how many nice colors you can make for the horses. Remember, keep your dots close together (A). Finally, place colorful dots over the two horses you painted a light black.

Select your two favorite colors for the horses and color the larger horses on the bottom of your *marker card* with dots. Can you have a light side and a shaded side? The light is coming from the right so that will be your light side. You can make it lighter by placing your dots farther apart or by adding more orange. For the shaded side, use more purple or brown, or place your dots closer together (B). Practice with your colored pencils in the picture on the bottom of page 112 before beginning.

Lesson #86: Marker Card #4

Place *Marker Card #4* in front of you. To begin, let's draw a *bit* and *bridle* on the horse's head. Do you remember how you did this in Lesson #25? Practice drawing this on the horse below (C) with your brown colored pencil. When you are finished, darken it in with your black colored pencil and then mix several colors together to create a nice color for your horse. Finally, can you complete the bottom of the picture frame? Use a ruler for the edges and your black pen, showing the wooden texture with short, broken lines, just as you did in Lesson #84.

C.

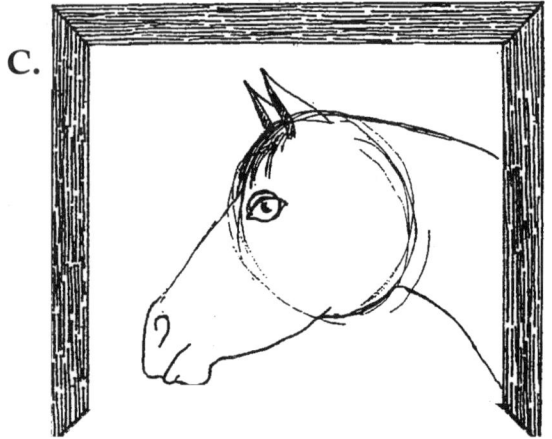

Draw a bit, bridle, and mane on the horse's head on the *marker card* with your yellow colored marker. Go over everything with your brown marker when finished. Then color his head and mane with any colored markers you like. Just for fun, color the other bridled horse in the picture frame next to it. You can color with dots, lines, or blending. Finally, complete the bottom of your frame with your black drawing pen. Next, draw the picture of the horse. First, lightly draw the horse in the large picture frame on the bottom of your *marker card* with your yellow colored pencil.

When you have finished, draw the fence in front of him and the hill, farm house, and trees in the distance with your yellow marker. Before beginning, complete the drawing in the smaller picture of the leaping horse by finishing the fence in the foreground and the details in the background. This will be a good practice before beginning your final picture. When you have it just right, go over everything with your black drawing pen. In the areas where one line goes over another (like the tail of the horse going through the fence), you can use white out to blot, or erase, that part of the tail.

Now you are ready to complete the drawing of the horse, fence, and farmland in the large figure box on the bottom of your *marker card*. Do you want to give your horse markings? Before continuing, color in the four circles on your *marker card* with your orange, brown, green, and blue colored markers. Then, dip your brush in water and rub it in the orange circle and paint your horse a light orange. Do this again by rubbing a wet brush in the brown to make a light brownish/orange for your horse. You may want to color over the mane with your yellow and orange markers and then blend the colors with a slightly wet brush. Finally, dip your brush in water one more time and rub it in the blue circle and paint a light blue sky. (Make sure to paint around any clouds in your sky.) Use your colored markers and color the fence with short, broken strokes of brown and orange to give it a nice texture. Color the field with your yellow colored marker. Then, dip a wet brush in the green circle and paint over the yellow field a light green. After you have finished coloring your picture and it has dried, you may want to take your black drawing pen and outline some areas for more detail.

Lesson #87: Marker Card #5

For our last marker assignment see how creative and colorful you can be! Place *Marker Card #5* in front of you. For this lesson we are going to do just as you did in Lesson #32. However, this time you are going to draw a larger picture and color it with markers. Our purpose for this lesson is to draw a horse and to camouflage him in the artwork so he is difficult to see. Again, notice the drawings by the two students (left).

Drawing by Marta Stolen Age 10   Kate Whitting Age 10

Let's start by doing a series of small drawings in the figure boxes on the next page, seeing how creatively you can merge, or blend in the horses, with the background. A good way to do this is by using *contour lines*. A contour line is one continuous line, moving in and out, over and under. Drawing like this will free you up and create some interesting patterns and designs. You can make your contour line like leaves (A), or like woodlands (B), like rocks (C), or anything else you like!

A.

B.

C.

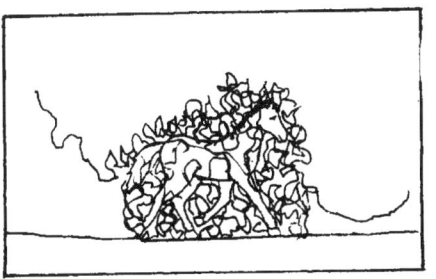
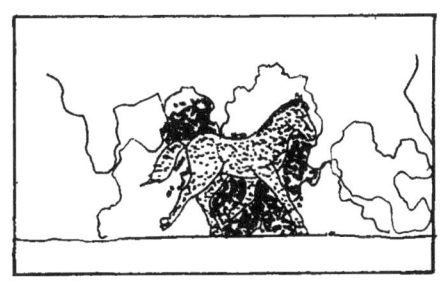

Notice that I have added creative backgrounds to partially conceal the delightful horses drawn by Rebekah Lorenz and Gray Goodner (below). Take your black drawing pen and complete the backgrounds, continuing to camouflage the horses. Then, create your own horse drawings in the nine figure boxes with creative backgrounds that will conceal them. Again, if you like, you can use contour lines. Remember, with a contour drawing it is one continuous line, going in and out, over and under. Don't forget to blend the horse into the background by having some of the background design go into the horse. Be creative! When you are finished, select your best picture and draw it large on Marker Card #5 with your yellow colored marker. Finally, before coloring it in with your colored markers. Practice some of your colors with your colored pencils in the pictures you create below. Use some of the techniques you have learned, like coloring with lines, dots, or blending to make your art work even more creative. Relax and be creative! Fill the entire picture with designs and patterns. Last of all, color in your picture using dots, lines, and blending. Then, see if someone can find your horse.

A Sad Story with a Happy Ending

"A Horse" by Alex Perry Age 6

Dear Students;

Well, we hope that you have enjoyed "The Wonderful Art of Drawing Horses!" I would love to hear from you, to see some of your horse drawings, and also to hear how you liked the book. Please write. We love receiving letters from you!

In closing I want to tell you a little sad story with a happy ending. Did you know that race horses often end their careers by being put to death. They are put through so many physical demands during their years of racing that their bodies become in very poor health. Some are sent to dog food factories and others are sent to other countries as food. Recently, many states have been taking these horses and starting horse farms for youths who have been having emotional problems. The program has met with great success as these youth now feel worthwhile in just being able to help a horse that is in need. And, of course, if someone treats a horse with love and tenderness then the horse is going to respond in the same manner. The program is so successful that they are expanding it to many other states. Even though some of these old race horses are being saved there are still many others that need a home! For more information and stories on these race horses you may want to plug in to the website: trfinc.org or call (859) 246-3080.
God bless you, and keep up the great work!
In Christ,

Stebbing

Barry Stebbing
How Great Thou ART Publications
Box 48
McFarlan, NC 28102
www.howgreatthouart.com

The End

"A Horse"
Heidi Hempel Age 12

Student Art Gallery

"In the Pasutre" by Don Fizure Age 45

"Wild Indian Pony" by Hannah Parrish Age 14

"The Colorado Ranger" by Kaylee Devantier Age 11

"Steed" by Kelsey Moore Age 13

"Pony" by Brianna Mason Age 11

"Stallion" by Helen Carlson Age 85

Student Art Gallery

"Beauty" by Emily Krogman Age 14

"Desert Ride" by Trevor Age 8

"Feeding Time" by Sidney Boyd Age 11

"Horse Stall" by Morgan McClanahan Age 14

"Mustang Pinto" by Mirriam Rose Parrish Age 11

"Horse & Rider" by Luke Andersen Age 8

The Wonderful Art of Drawing Horses

Sketchbook

"Strive to become an artist and the rest will take care of itself." Shuman

Keeping a Sketchbook

Sketchbooks are wonderful to have. A sketchbook is an easy way to keep all your drawings together, it can make a nice display or portfolio of your artwork, and is easy to travel with. When keeping a sketchbook it is recommended that you fill your pages, even if you make a mistake. A full page makes for a nice presentation and also allows you to economize. It is also recommended that you use *figure boxes* for some of your drawings, as this makes a nice frame for your sketches and also a more pleasing composition. Figure boxes can be of any size (A) and some have been provided for you to sketch in on the first page of your sketchbook.

A.

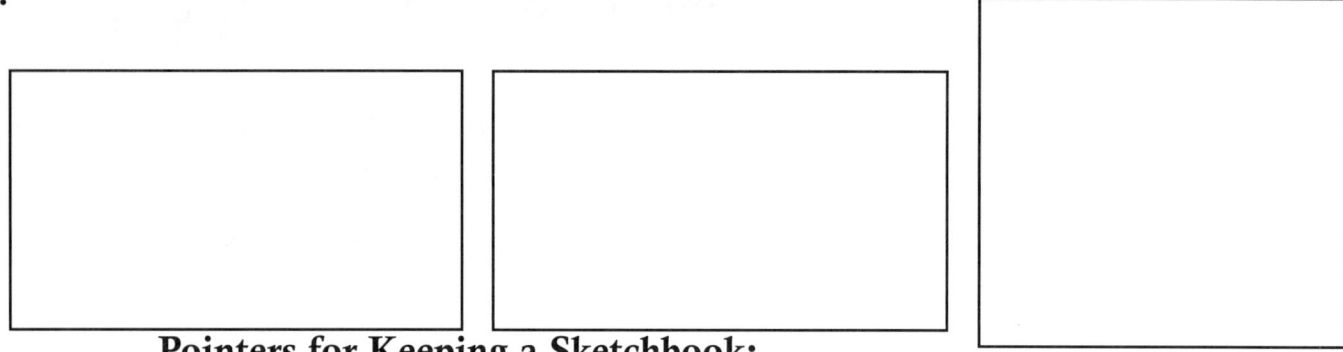

Pointers for Keeping a Sketchbook:

1. Fill Your Pages With Drawings
2. Use Figure Boxes for some of Your Drawings

Pointers for Drawing

Several pointers to know in beginning drawing. First of all, always sharpen your pencils. It is very important to draw with a nice point. Try to practice drawing everyday. Remember, the more you practice, the better you will become. Go to the library and copy drawings by the masters. This is a great way to learn drawing techniques. It is also recommended that you draw from "life," or objects that are around you. Start your drawings off lightly. With drawing pencils this means starting with your lightest pencil (an "H" or an "HB" pencil). Try to refrain from using an eraser as many students erase too much and it can take away from your confidence as an artist. Likewise, refrain from using a ruler and learn how to draw nice, controlled lines freehand. If you need to know if there is anything wrong with your drawing hold it up to a mirror. This will give you a reverse image and point out many of your mistakes.

Pointers for Drawing:

1. Sharpen Pencils
2. Practice Everyday
3. Copy the Masters
4. Draw from Life
5. Start off Lightly
6. Refrain from Erasing
7. Refrain from Rulers
8. Hold Drawing in front of Mirror

What Do You Recommend Next?

Now that you have finished *I Can Do All Things,* How Great Thou ART Publications would like to introduce you to many other delightful art books that you may want to study from next. For example, if you are still under the age of ten, we recommend *Lambs I & II Books of Art* or *The Wonderful Art of Drawing Horses.* If you are now over the age of ten and really like art, then we recommend a great art book, *Feed My Sheep.* Below is a brief description of each. For other curriculum, videos, and bundle packages see next page.

Feed My Sheep   Ages 10 & Up

This best selling curriculum is a comprehensive art text and workbook containing over 250, illustrated, step-by-step lessons. The recommended weaving in and out of the chapters will provide the student with a little drawing, painting, penmanship, art appreciation, etc...during any given month. Over 300 pages in a spiralbound, softcover text includes 17 heavy cardstock paint cards.

4 Year Curriculum
Ask about our Bundle Package!
(includes text, paints & brushes, colored pencils, black drawing pen, drawing pencil set, sharpener, and kneaded eraser)

God & the History of ART   Ages 10 & Up

A great resource, this four year curriculum features an extensive survey of art history, supplemented with over 250 art lessons teaching beginning drawing, painting, colored markers, perspective, color theory and much more. Text also includes a set of 35 *paint cards* for the painting assignments and a set of 34 full color post cards of works by the great masters. *God & the History of ART* focuses on those periods of art that strived to glorify God, such as Early Christian, Byzantine, Gothic, etc.

A 4 Year Curriculum
Ask about our Bundle Package!
(includes text, paints & brushes, colored pencils, #7 brush, set of 8 colored markers, black drawing pen, drawing pencil set, sharpener, and kneaded eraser)

Lambs Book of Art I & II   Ages 8 thru 13

These award winning, one-year curriculum have been a favorite with homeschooling families for years and are a delightful introduction to art. Subjects include color theory, drawing, anatomy, perspective, nature studies, portraits, cartooning, lettering, creative writing, and much more. The Lambs Book of Art II complements Lamb's I with more lessons on the same level and you can start with each or use both to extend your program.

A 1 year curriculum

Order Today! 1-800-982 DRAW (3729)

How Great Thou Art Publications Presents...
Barry Stebbing's Complete ART Curriculum

Ages 3 Thru 13

Baby Lambs Book of Art
(Ages 3 Thru 5)

Not a coloring book! Teaches beginning drawing, beginning color theory, beginning lettering, beginning addition and subtraction, and beginning writing - all in a fun way with art! Over 128 pages 8 1/2" x 11"

Joseph the Canada Goose

Children ages 4 thru 8 will love this delightful story about a Canada goose with a broken wing named Joseph and his relationship with a lonely old farmer named Elmer Thatcher. What makes this book unique is that every page has an art lesson to go with it. Text includes 100 pages with over 45 art lessons. Recommended materials are a set of colored pencils & a black drawing pen.
•Bundle Package! Text, Prismacolor colored pencils, and a fine black drawing pen all for 1 low price!

Little Annie's Art Book of Etiquette & Good Manners
(Ages 4 Thru 9)

An adorable text that teaches the social graces with scripture along with simple art assignments. Lessons on dinner etiquette, being a good listener, saying "Please and Thank You," obeying your parents, writing thank you cards, refinement, spending quality time away from the television and much more! All with fun and easy art lessons.

The Children's Art Journal

This text is recommended for students ages 6 thru 10. This text offers 50 basic art lessons teaching fundamentals of drawing & color theory along with a 70 page beginning journal in the back of the text. Journaling encourages good penmanship and helps.

I Can Do All Things
(Ages 6 Thru 11)

A Basic Beginning Art Book! Learn to draw, color and paint with these easy step by step lessons. A complete curriculum with over 250 pages and 170 art lessons, includes 38 8 1/2" x 11" paint & Marker cards.
• **Supplies for ICD:** Paints & Brushes, 12 "Prismacolor" Colored Pencils, Watercolor Markers, # 7 Brush, Fine Pen, Kneaded Eraser & Sharpener.

I Can Do All Things Video
Over seven hours of instruction in a four tape series covering most of the lessons in the text. Includes an "I Can Do All Things" book.
• **Video Bundle Package!** Same as above Bundle plus 4 Video Set.

Now Available on DVD!
The same great teaching aid now on 4 menu driven DVD's.

Lamb's Book of Art I
(Ages 8 Thru 13)

Teaches a well rounded foundation in art. Subjects include color theory, drawing, perspective, nature studies, anatomy, portraits, cartooning, lettering, creative writing and more.

Lamb's Book of Art II

to instill creativity in your children. Lamb's Book of ART II. A continuation of Lamb's Book of Art I. Over 70 Daily Lessons.

Lamb's Book I Video
Great teaching tool! Over 4 hours of instruction. Covers the 70 lessons in the Lamb's Book of Art I. Barry demonstrates how to use color, draw cartoons, learn perspective, study nature and much more. Three tape series includes a Lamb's Book I.
Inquire about DVD's

Ages 8 Thru Adult

The Wonderful Art of Drawing Horses
(Ages 8 Thru Adult)

Homeschooling children love to draw horses! What better way to teach students the fundamentals of drawing & color theory than by having them draw and color one of God's most beautiful creations. This text has been written for those students who have the desire & determination to draw horses correctly (and learn a little about them along the way)! Lessons may be done directly in the text or copied for in-home use. For Ages 8 & Up / Over 75 daily lessons.
•**Special Bundle Package!** Text, sketchbook, "Prismacolor" colored pencils, fine black pen, drawing pencil set, pencil sharpener & kneaded eraser.

God & The History of Art
A Godly Perspective to Art History
(Ages 10 Thru Adult)

Learn drawing, painting and art history at the same time! God & The History of Art focuses on those periods of art that strived to glorify God such as Early Christian, Byzantine, Romanesque, Gothic, and Early Renaissance. God & The History of Art is filled with art lessons that complement the period of time, or artist, that is being studied. Examinations cover each period of art. The art lessons teach basic fundamentals in drawing, painting, and color theory. A great program for a well rounded education in art.

Also Available for God & the History
•**Additional Paint & Marker Cards**
(Recommended one set per student)
•**Supplies for God & History:** Paints & Brushes, 12 "Prismacolor" Colored Pencils, Watercolor Markers, # 7 Brush, Ultra Fine Pen, Drawing Pencil Set, Kneaded Eraser & Sharpener.

Feed My Sheep
(Ages 10 Thru Adult)
An Art Curriculum that will last for years!
•Over 100 lessons just on Beginning Drawing
•A practical course in Art appreciation
•Beginning paint lessons •Nature Studies
•Perspective •Penmanship •Academia
•Anatomy • Portraits
Over 300 pages 8 1/2" x 11"
Also Available for Feed My Sheep
Additional Paint Cards (Recommended one set per student)
Supplies for FMS: Paints & Brushes, 12 "Prismacolor" Colored Pencils, Ultra Fine Pen, Drawing Pencil Set, Kneaded Eraser & Sharpener.
Paint Cards Included Not just paint by numbers! Barry Stebbing has constructed a series of seventeen (17) educational and enjoyable painting exercises. Each is on a sturdy 8 1/2" x 11" white poster board ready for painting!

Feed My Sheep Videos
Over nine hours of instruction in a seven video series instructed by artist/teacher Barry Stebbing. Learn drawing and painting, nature studies, portraits, perspective and more! A must for every serious art student! Includes a Feed My Sheep text with Paint Cards
Video Bundle Package! Text w/paint cards, & video set plus all the art supplies needed to complete this 4 year course.

Feed My Sheep is now available on DVD!
The same great teaching aid now on 7 menu driven DVD's.

Ages 10 Thru Adult

The Student's Guide to Keeping an Art Journal
(Ages 10 Thru Adult)

Did you know that Leonardo da Vinci completed over 5,000 journal pages in his lifetime? Journaling is a wonderful & creative way to help your children improve their drawing and writing skills. Beginning a journal course will also help to instill creativity in your children by encouraging them to do independent studies and to draw from life! In the Students Guide to Keeping an Art Journal, Barry discusses what to write about, what to draw, having a theme, and much more as he invites students into the world of art Journaling. This newly revised text also includes over 40 art lessons.

How Great Thou ART I
(Ages 13 Thru Adult)

Teaches a strong foundation in Art: learning the basics of drawing, especially drawing from life. Subjects include: beginning drawing, anatomy, portraits, pen and ink, nature studies, perspective, graphics and more. Students can work directly in text. Sketchbook included in back. Over 65 daily Lessons / Over 100 pages 8 1/2" x 11".

How Great Thou ART II
(Ages 13 Thru Adult)

A complementary ART text for How Great Thou ART I. Does not matter which text you start with, simply more daily lessons in beginning drawing, pen and ink, perspective, nature studies, graphics and more. Also includes an introduction to lettering and calligraphy.

How Great Thou ART I & II Video
Anyone Can Learn To Draw!
(Over 4 1/2 hours of instruction in 3 tapes)
Learn To Draw! Covers the lessons in How Great Thou ART I & II on beginning drawing, especially from life. Barry goes over many of the fundamentals of drawing such as: line, ellipse, axis line, values, shading, light source, proportions, anatomy, perspective, portraits and much more! A must for every student serious about drawing. Includes both books. **Inquire about DVD's**

Teacher's Manual...
For How Great Thou ART I & II
The How Great Thou ART I & II manual has been created to give thorough guidance and instruction for each lesson in the two texts. The manual will give the teacher a thorough understanding of many of the finer nuances that go into instruction of the assignments.

Book of Many Colors
(Ages 12 Thru Adult)

Learn all about color through the use of colored pencils, markers, pastels, watercolors, oils and acrylics! This book has over 250 pages and includes 30 8 1/2" x 11" heavy index Paint & Marker cards. A great book for anyone serious about color theory & painting.

The Book of Many Colors Video Set
(Ages 12 Thru Adult)
Finally a video set designed for the Homeschooling family that focuses on color theory and painting! The videos compliment the Book of Many Colors text and cover many of its assignments. Over 4 hours of instruction in a three video set which includes the Book of Many Colors text.
Inquire about DVD's

Satisfaction Guaranteed! To order call **Toll Free:**
1.800.982.DRAW(3729)
See Our Monthly Specials At:
www.howgreatthouart.com
How Great Thou Art Box 48 McFarlan, NC 28102